# Life by Pumpkin

Book 4

# *The Bark Diaries*

# Life by Pumpkin

Book 4

# *The Bark Diaries*

Leslie Popp

Copyright © 2026 Leslie Popp

All rights reserved. No part of this book may be reproduced or used in any manner without written permission of the copyright owner except for the use of quotations in a book review.

First hardcover edition May 2026

Book design by Leslie Popp

ISBN-13: 979-8-9947195-1-0

In loving memory of Rachel and Sara, whose slobbery smiles and enthusiastic wags will never be forgotten. The following tales depict real events from the pups' point of view. I hope they brighten your day as much as they brightened our lives.

- Leslie

# Table of Contents

| | |
|---|---|
| Introduction by Rachel | 1 |
| Introduction by Sara | 5 |
| Homecoming | 10 |
| Mississippi to New Hampshire | 15 |
| Momma's Girl | 23 |
| Boundaries | 28 |
| A Beginner's Guide to Demanding Back Rubs | 34 |
| Kibble vs. Pizza | 39 |
| The Thing About Toys | 47 |
| The Art of Shedding | 51 |
| Neighborhood Patrol | 56 |
| Itty Bitty Visitor | 62 |
| Finders Keepers | 69 |
| Where There is Rain, There Are Puddles | 76 |
| I Decline Rainy Days | 82 |
| The Park Downstairs | 90 |
| We Love to Pawty | 98 |
| Please Hand Me My Food | 104 |
| Field Trips and Felines | 110 |
| Bath Time | 118 |
| Vanilla Cupcakes | 124 |
| Dancing and Kisses | 133 |
| Chariot Ride | 138 |

| | |
|---|---|
| Family Huddle | 145 |
| His Majesty | 152 |
| Mom's Assistant | 160 |
| Road Trip | 166 |
| Our New Happy Home | 173 |
| My Friend Pumpkin | 180 |
| Beach Vibes | 187 |
| Pumpkin Sets the Record Straight | 194 |
| Author's Bio | 199 |
| Rachel's and Sara's Bios | 200 |
| Pumpkin's Bio | 201 |
| Synopsis | 202 |
| Quotes and Reviews | 203 |

## Introduction by Rachel

Hello, I'm so excited to meet you! After observing the excitement around my big brother Pumpkin's *Life by Pumpkin* series, I thought it was time to share my own story. There's nothing I love more than meeting people who adore animals, and I can't wait to learn more about you. While I'm a shy pup by nature, writing is the perfect way for me to make new friends.

The world is a fascinating place, and I'll do my best to relay my experiences as a sandy-colored Labrador Retriever mix. I hope your furry companion is curled up by your side or at your feet while you read. The quiet moments when we're snuggled up with our favorite human are the highlights of our lives as loyal pets.

If you don't have a dog but have wanted one forever, then you should pause here, hurry to your local animal shelter, and adopt a pet that can nap beside you while you enjoy my tales of adorable animal antics. I'll take an afternoon snooze while you're away, so just scratch the itchy spot behind my ears when you're ready to continue reading.

# Leslie Popp

Welcome back, and congratulations on adopting a new four-legged family member or members! Rescuing a pet in need is a rewarding experience, and I hope that every shelter animal finds a loving forever home.

Maybe you can read these chapters aloud so the furry members of your family can enjoy the story or simply listen to the sound of your voice. I hate to admit it, but dogs can't read, and it's a shame that my canine cousins will never be able to interpret these pages. That being said, many dogs will benefit from their owners learning valuable techniques to properly spoil their pooches. I advocate for lavishing love and affection on your dog—I can't stress that enough. We love you unconditionally and only desire attention, walks in the sunshine, and bountiful bowls of food and water.

Given most dogs are illiterate, due to the shocking lack of doggy schools to teach us this valuable skill, you may be wondering how I managed to write a book. This is an excellent question and something I had to grapple with when embarking on this project.

The first challenge was that my paws were either too small or too large to operate Mom's laptop. My toes are less agile than your fingers, and I struggle to press individual keys. I end up hitting multiple letters, which makes it difficult to type a specific word, let alone spell it correctly. The pads of my feet are not equipped to stretch across the keyboard, and it was discouraging to discover that my first paragraph was a jumble of letters and symbols. At that point, I almost gave up hope, but Mom came to the rescue.

# The Bark Diaries

Understanding that I was frustrated and unable to use the magic laptop machine, Mom situated herself at the professional-looking desk and began to type, diligently recording my adventures. I stood by her side, rested my head on her lap, and dictated page after page until chapters began to take shape. I would periodically lick her elbow as a thank you for assisting in my hour of need. When my paws grew tired of standing, I would wedge myself under the desk and keep Mom's feet warm to ensure she was comfortable and had optimal conditions for documenting my stories.

Once the initial draft was completed, we snuggled up on the couch to meticulously review the manuscript. She read it aloud, marking the pages with a red pen to record our clever edits before returning to the laptop to implement the changes. This process was repeated several times before we were satisfied with the final product.

Next, we had to create the cover art, which was a daunting task, and I'm still unsure how I feel about it. We sifted through hundreds of photos, and I even posed for a few more, before narrowing the options and asking Dad's opinion on the final selection.

The first copy was printed and delivered to us for approval. I was overjoyed but also felt skeptical about having my face on the cover. Was I the right pup for the job? Maybe I should remain anonymous, and we could use a professional model for the photo. The thought of everyone seeing my wet nose and floppy ears made me feel nervous. Mom and Sara assured me that I was perfect from nose to tail, and Mom explained that I deserved the credit for my hard work. My heart soared as I realized she was right; this was my story, and I was the only one who could tell it. I approved the final draft of the book, and we sent it to print.

I'm excited to share my adventures, and I hope that they make you smile. Mom reads a chapter to me every night before going to bed, and I can almost recite them by heart.

# The Bark Diaries

## Introduction by Sara

Greetings, wonderful humans! I'm so glad to meet you and attempt to lick each one of your smiling faces. I hope that you like slobbery kisses because they're my specialty.

After conferring with my big brother, Pumpkin, and my sister from another mister, Rachel, I decided it was high time for me to write my story and share it with you lovely readers. Writing is a new pursuit for me, since I usually spend my days curled up on the couch, trotting around the neighborhood, begging for food, and snuggling with Mom and Dad. There's so much that I want to tell you, and I don't know where to start.

First, I want to thank you for giving me your full attention. I love being the center of attention and having new friends pet my back and rub my belly. You're welcome to do both if you live nearby or are ever in the area. Stop by anytime because I maintain an open-door policy for animal lovers, especially if they come bearing treats. Chewy morsels are my favorite, but I'm willing to eat just about anything if you offer it to me from your hand.

Second, I hope that any furry friends in your household aren't jealous that you're reading a book about a Golden Retriever you've never met. Not every dog can write a novel, and my story is meant to be fun and uplifting for everyone. I would never want another animal to feel left out or resentful because their owner is interested in me. Tell your pet to talk to my mom if they want their story published. My mom loves animals and hands out belly rubs and treats like it's her job.

Lastly, if you don't have a pet, then I would encourage you to drop what you're doing and head to your local animal shelter to rescue a new friend. There are countless dogs like Rachel and me and cats like Pumpkin that need loving homes. They're just waiting for you to peer into their cages and fall in love. Trust me, being a pet parent is an incredibly rewarding experience and will bring joy and love into your life. If you already have a pet, then you can always adopt a second, third, or fourth fur baby. I don't discriminate between dogs and cats, so any pet is fine with me, except for pigeons; I chase pigeons.

You might wonder about my motivations for writing this tale and how I developed my writing skills. I spent several years watching my brother, Pumpkin, as he launched his feline-focused novels, taking the notoriety in stride and making it look effortless. Then my sister, Rachel, began drafting a few chapters, which was a huge challenge given her timid personality. Initially, she lacked confidence in her writing and worried about what readers would think. With support from our family, she completed her side of the story and felt ready to publish it. I convinced her to pose for the cover photo after she claimed that she wasn't cute enough, which is nonsense because Rachel is adorable. However, I knew that our story would be incomplete without including my version of events.

I had no experience with writing, so I set out to learn what I could before making the decision to compose my side of the story. However, when I sat down beside Mom's desk and stared at the laptop that she was always clacking away on, I realized that the device was at eye level, and my paws couldn't reach the keys. On top of that, the laptop was closed and failed to respond to my mental commands. I was stumped and stared at the machine, wondering how to open it and turn it on. I understood the basic operation of the device, which involved tapping the black keys while staring intently at the glowing screen. I wasn't sure how the computer absorbed ideas and translated them into the pages of a book, but I'm a smart pup and was confident that if Rachel and Pumpkin could figure it out, then so could I. I wasn't worried.

Tilting my head to one side and then the other didn't help, and I quickly lost interest and found myself gazing out the window at the cars zooming by. Eventually, my mom wondered where I had wandered off to and came looking for me. I wagged my tail enthusiastically as she entered the room, patted my head, and took a seat in front of the computer. Finally, help had arrived and we were back in business. I wedged myself under the desk and rested my head on her lap, my wet nose pressing against her thigh as I gazed up at her with wide eyes.

## Leslie Popp

I was so glad she was there to assist in this challenging process, and I knew that together we would bring my story to life. As I raised my eyebrows and focused on telepathically communicating the opening sentence to Mom, I was rewarded with the familiar clacking of the magical keys. The screen wasn't visible from my position, but I felt confident that Mom was correctly transcribing my ideas. The sentences began to flow effortlessly, and we stayed like that for hours, reveling in our creative genius. Occasionally, I became distracted by thoughts of food, but I tried to remain focused.

When the book was finished, we put our heads together to edit early copies and made the necessary revisions. I accidentally drooled on a few pages, but Mom didn't mind, and it certainly didn't bother me.

Next, it was picture time. Mom and I planted ourselves in front of the computer and sifted through folders filled with my likenesses, examining each one and editing our favorites. She made them brighter, enhanced the color, and cropped out anyone in the background. I love Dad, but this is my book, and I couldn't allow him to photobomb my cover image.

Finally, a copy of the finished product arrived in the mail, and we jumped around excitedly before settling in to scrutinize it for any defects. I saw the shaggy face on the cover and wondered who it was before remembering that it was me. Then I hopped around and thought, "I'm on the cover of a book! Look, that's me!"

Once I calmed down, we examined each page and scrutinized every aspect. I thought it was marvelous, but I appreciated Mom's eye for design and detail. I wanted my novel to be perfect and impress my audience. When Mom was satisfied, and I had thoroughly sniffed the composition, we signed off and sent the precious work out into the world to bring joy to humans and their furry companions. I hope that the story makes my readers laugh and leads to many new friends who enjoy slobbery kisses.

Leslie Popp

*Rachel*

## Homecoming

Mississippi was too hot for my thick straw-colored fur. I can't remove my fluffy covering the way humans can shed their layers of fabric. The air was humid, and the sun was unforgiving, particularly during the summer. Most of my time was spent tethered to a post outside, and I longed for an owner that was loving and attentive, but this way of life was all I had ever known, and I had learned to be grateful for the small things. At least I had my older sister, Sara, a shaggy Golden Retriever with a perpetual smile. It was just the two of us, and we couldn't imagine life without each other.

Let's fast forward to the year I turned six, and Sara turned seven. After some difficulties in our first home, we were fostered on a blueberry farm in New Hampshire, which was very different from where we grew up. Our host family owned a beautiful plot of land and a wonderful home that we soon settled into. They led us on hikes to enjoy the fresh air and see the countryside, but we weren't accustomed to that level of activity, so we would lie down after a few minutes and refuse to walk any further. This forced us all to turn around and head home for snacks and an afternoon nap.

Our insistence on short walks was due to Sara's disabled front leg, which was the result of an old injury that wasn't properly treated by our original owners. She learned to walk on three legs and never fully regained use of the fourth. I don't like to talk about that time in our lives and prefer to focus on our more promising future. Sara's physical limitations prevented her from engaging in strenuous activities like hiking, but they never stopped her from sharing affection with our foster family. The two of us were inseparable. If she needed to relax, so would I.

One sunny day, a brown-haired man and his friend rumbled down our driveway in a large vehicle and greeted us warmly. Our foster parents were excited to meet the man and encouraged us to say hello. We obliged, and I liked him from the start because he was gentle and spoke enthusiastically while petting us. We bonded with him immediately and understood that he was an animal person with a kind heart. Dogs are adept at reading people, and my instincts have never led me astray. I was delighted to cozy up next to this newcomer, despite being shy and reserved. Sara returned his affection twice over while wagging her tail so hard that she accidentally smacked me across the face, forcing me to step back. The man showed us equal attention while noticing my nervousness and trying to reassure me.

He hoisted us into the back of a spacious vehicle, and we drove away from the farm. I watched the blueberries recede into the distance, wondering about our destination and what lay ahead. Car rides were always exciting, and I loved watching the world zoom by while the other cars jockeyed for the spot beside us. There's something magical about moving at high speeds, and I wished we could lower the back window so I could stick my head out and enjoy the cool breeze on my nose.

Admittedly, I was also nervous about traveling to an unknown location with a relative stranger. I liked the man, but everything was new to me, and I was apprehensive about our next home. Was he aware that we needed kibble and went on daily walks? While we only lived with the family in New Hampshire for a brief time, they were kind to me, and I was certain they wouldn't let an unfriendly person take me away.

I waited anxiously to arrive at my new home, pondering a range of scenarios, including returning to Mississippi or living in a loving home with friendly people, soft places to nap, and abundant food and water. I hoped for the latter because that is every dog's dream.

We arrived in a big city, and the sound of honking horns echoed through the streets. I was in awe of the lights and the sheer number of people and cars. The buildings stretched up to the sky, and I wondered how humans climbed to the top.

The car stopped in front of a brick building, and the man helped us down to the ground and looped colorful leashes around our necks so we couldn't wander into the street. There were many intriguing scents, and my nose struggled to process them as they wafted over me on the afternoon breeze. I smelled delightful cooking from a restaurant down the street, the exhaust from passing cars, new leaves on the tree sprouting up from the sidewalk, and the scents of other dogs who have walked this route. Apparently, many animals called this neighborhood home, and I hoped the residents were friendly.

The change of scenery was daunting, and I was scared and overwhelmed. I stared at the ground for a moment, letting my head hang low and taking slow breaths to calm my racing heart. Sensing my anxiety, the man leaned down and gently tousled my fur, which did wonders to reassure me. Sara appeared to be enjoying herself and was busy scanning the area and sniffing enthusiastically to map our new territory. With an encouraging word and a friendly smile, the man guided us through the building and into a metal elevator that dinged as the doors whooshed open. We emerged into a carpeted hallway, and the man fumbled with a key to open one of the identical doors, giving us the first look at our forever home.

The entry room was cheery with bright lights, a cozy blue couch, and the aroma of spicy food lingering in the air. The two men welcomed us and encouraged us to explore the rooms at our leisure. To my delight, they set out bowls of dry food and cool water for us to quench our thirst and snack at our discretion. Food makes everything better, and I felt that our new friends understood me.

I'm uneasy in unfamiliar locations and felt nervous while wandering around. I was fearful that danger could be lurking around every corner, so I initially stayed in the entry room, which was a safe space. I spent several long minutes staring at the ground and feeling overwhelmed. I didn't know the rules of this house, and I was afraid to make a mistake that would upset the delicate bond I had established with the man.

Suddenly, he was by my side, gently patting my head and beckoning for me to proceed into the next room. Mustering my courage, I timidly followed him, hoping that I was behaving like an obedient dog. I tried to look adorable and sweet because this seemed like a happy place, and I wanted to live here forever.

The man sat on the couch and extended both hands. I paused and assessed the situation, while my sister barreled over and reveled in the attention. I returned my gaze to the floor, afraid that I had missed my opportunity. Then I heard him gently call my name, Rachel, and it gave me the courage to cross the room. He held one hand out for me to sniff while continuing to pet Sara, who was gazing at him adoringly. Hesitantly, I leaned my head against his knee, allowing him to rub my back. The motion was soothing, and my heartbeat settled into a normal rhythm.

I sighed in relief because we were truly welcome here. I had always wanted a loving family, and now I had finally found one.

## *Sara*

### Mississippi to New York

Mississippi temperatures were tough; it has the kind of heat that you can't beat by panting; trust me, I know. My thick, golden fur is meant to keep me toasty on winter days as I romp through the snow and is not ideal for warm climates. Even my constant shedding couldn't cool me down in the searing summer heat and stifling humidity. I spent my first seven years in that sweltering state, but I don't like to think about those early days.

My first family failed to care for me properly, and I spent most of my time chained in the yard without much human interaction. Luckily, I had Rachel for company, and we helped each other through the tough times. She is a Yellow Labrador Retriever mix, and I am a Golden Retriever, so we're not technically sisters, but we've been together since puppyhood, and we might as well be related. Rachel is my soul sister, and we're bonded for life. I can't imagine being separated from her, even for a few hours.

Rachel and I spent the long Mississippi days wondering if all humans adopted dogs only to neglect their parenting duties. When we grew bored of lounging around, we would chew on our heavy chains, which slowly wore down my beautiful teeth until they were stubby and flat. I wanted to roam the yard and wondered if that was too much to hope for.

Then one day, I sustained an injury to my front leg, and despite being unable to place any weight on that paw, my owners failed to rush me to a professional for proper treatment. I hate the vet as much as the next dog, but in that instance, I desperately needed the aid of a healthcare specialist. Rachel did her best to support and encourage me while I recovered at home, but she lacked medical training and couldn't mend the damage. Still, I appreciated her concern and took comfort in her proximity.

My leg eventually healed, but I still walk with a pronounced limp, relying on my other three limbs to support my weight and using my injured appendage only for balance. While it was difficult, I tried to maintain a positive attitude and adjust to my new way of life. Now, let's jump forward a few years to a happier time.

My first foster home, a blueberry farm in New Hampshire, was a cheerful place with lovely people who showered me with affection. The climate was cooler, which was a major improvement over my prior situation. The area was picturesque, with clean air, lush vegetation, and an abundance of open space. I was a country dog now without any chains holding me back.

My disabled leg made attending the family hikes difficult, and after only a few minutes, I would lie down, feeling exhausted from the challenging footing and the exertion. The kind people were accommodating, but as it turns out, this relocation was only a temporary home for us until a permanent family was found. We eventually gave up on the hikes and settled for calmer activities, which was fine by me because I preferred to take long naps on the couch and plead for affection. Who wants to walk up rocky hills for great views anyway?

Rachel and I didn't have to wait long for our forever family, and one day an unfamiliar vehicle rumbled up the driveway and paused in front of the house. Two men emerged from the car, and I watched with anticipation. Who could these strangers be?

Our foster family greeted the visitors warmly and encouraged Rachel and me to come outside. I didn't need much convincing to meet new friends. I limped forward, sniffing the newcomers and contemplating their unique scents. I investigated their shoes, shorts, hands, and even their backsides. They were friendly and spoke kindly to us, which immediately earned my affection.

The man with brown hair chatted happily with our foster parents while scratching me behind my ears. I licked his legs and leaned into his touch as my sign of approval. I hoped that he would stay and curl up with me on the couch. We could spend long afternoons together, and he could rub my belly while I drifted off into a peaceful nap. The thought warmed my heart, and I nuzzled his hand, wanting him to like me and never leave.

Rachel is timid and frightens easily, given our rough puppyhood, but she took to the brown-haired man as well. She stood close to him, keeping her head down obediently and staring meekly at the ground while he affectionately stroked her back. I could tell that she liked him and was pleased with his caring demeanor.

Little did we know, he was here to take us to the big city where we would start a new life. Rachel and I were loaded into the car, and we shared a nervous look, wondering about our destination. I hoped it wasn't a trip to the vet because I had long ago learned to walk on three legs and never wanted to see the vet again. We both loved car rides, so the unexpected trip was exciting. I couldn't help but pant heavily and gaze out the windows in wonder as we left the blueberry farm behind and zipped along sprawling highways lined with towering trees. I pressed my nose to the glass, watching the world fly by and trying to memorize our route. My internal compass rotated, but we soon exceeded my fifteen-minute walking radius from the house, and I lost track of the turns. No matter, these seemed like decent people, and I was sure they would take excellent care of us.

The brown-haired man called my name, and I swiveled my head in his direction, my floppy ears automatically tilting toward his voice. I excitedly waited for him to call my name again because I loved the way it sounded.

Given her cautious nature, Rachel was more skeptical about the situation. We're complete opposites where this is concerned; I'm carefree and greet every day with a smile, and she's quiet and always worried.

I love car rides, and I enjoyed the journey. The hours flew by as we rumbled down wood-lined roads, through quaint towns, and sped along crowded highways. I panted happily, hoping that our destination would have snacks and a bowl of cool water. My mouth was dry, and while my stomach was full of butterflies, a handful of treats sounded appealing. The sun traversed the blue sky, and it was a bit toasty in the back of the car, but I was used to warm weather after all those years in Mississippi.

We meandered through the crowded streets of a bustling city, pausing beside other vehicles at bright red lights. I peered at the car stopped behind us and gave the driver a welcoming smile in case he was friendly and wanted to pet me. I didn't know anyone in this area and would've been pleased to make his acquaintance. We continued along in heavy traffic, and I greeted every driver in the adjacent vehicles. Some smiled and acknowledged me, and others stared straight ahead, unaware of my presence or choosing to ignore me. I assumed they didn't notice me because people who dislike dogs cannot be trusted.

Our car veered off the main road and stopped in front of a lovely building with flowers sprouting along the sidewalk. The man with brown hair helped Rachel and me down from our seats and looped the colorful leashes over our heads. I gazed around in wonder.

The noise from cars honking and sirens blaring assaulted my ears, while the sounds of people laughing and birds chirping in the tree overhead floated by on the breeze. A host of new smells greeted my nose, and I zeroed in on a nearby pile of garbage baking in the sun, the markings of neighborhood dogs on the light pole, exhaust from the endless parade of cars, and the aroma of greasy food. Was that melted cheese and fresh bread that I detected? I hoped so! The experience was a sensory overload, and I tried to focus on one thing at a time.

The street was one block from the main road and lined with trees surrounded by flowers. The buildings were so tall that I had to stretch my neck to see how far they extended into the sky. I considered whether I could reach out and touch the puffy clouds from the roofs, and then I wondered if clouds were edible and what they tasted like. I hoped to find out.

The man led us to a glass door, and I was anxious to see our new home. The tile in the lobby was cold against my paws, and the surface was slick. My disabled leg compromised my balance, and I was conscious of my footing. I didn't want to trip over my feet in front of these new friends and look like a total klutz. I'm an able-bodied Golden Retriever capable of walking without assistance.

We boarded a fancy elevator, and the man checked that my tail was clear of the door before it closed with a whooshing sound. The box began to ascend, making a dinging noise at each floor. The anticipation was heavy in the air, and my panting sped up as my heart pounded nervously. Rachel sat quietly by my side, looking around warily, and I reassured her that everything would be alright if we stuck together. We had been through so much already, and I was optimistic about this place.

We exited into a carpeted hallway and paused in front of a heavy door, which the man flung open. We proceeded into a cheery-looking room with a large couch that was ideal for napping.

## The Bark Diaries

The man removed our leashes and tousled the fur on the tops of our heads. I gave his hand a hearty lick, ensuring it was extra slobbery so he would know how much I appreciated the attention. He hurried to fill a bowl with water and held it in front of my nose, and I began to lap up the cool liquid, enjoying the feel on my parched tongue. Rachel slowly approached, and after a moment of hesitation, began to drink. A few drops splattered on the floor, and I stared down at them, hoping that spilling wasn't a punishable offense. The man ignored my minor infraction and offered us a bowl of kibble.

I inspected the uniform morsels, noting the alluring smells of sweet potato and rice. It was a different brand than we typically ate, but I've never been a picky eater. In fact, I'll eat just about anything. I took a few delicate bites, not wanting to appear greedy or messy on my first day. I aimed to please and wanted my new friend to see that I was a wonderful addition to his house. The unfamiliar setting put a damper on my appetite, and I suddenly lost interest in the meal. Rachel nibbled a few pieces before looking up at the man.

He dropped to his knees and gently petted my neck while scratching Rachel behind her ears. I stepped toward him and sniffed his face, debating whether to plant a wet kiss on his cheek. I decided against it for now and quietly rejoiced at the attention. The new home seemed like a safe place, and I really liked the man. I had always wanted a loving dad, and perhaps I had finally found one. I couldn't wait to spend long afternoons lounging on the couch by his side, begging for belly rubs, and resting my head on his lap. This was the start of my wonderful new life.

## Rachel

### Momma's Girl

A few days after arriving at our new home, the woman of my dreams appeared in the doorway, and I was in love from the moment I laid eyes on her warm smile.

I was standing awkwardly near the couch, debating whether I was allowed to hop onto the soft cushions and curl up into a ball for an afternoon nap. The space looked cozy, and the two men obviously enjoyed sitting there, so I wanted to do the same. If we each occupied one cushion, then I could lie between them and solicit belly rubs from both, which seemed like a convenient strategy that I was determined to implement. First, I needed to confirm that the couch was a dog-friendly area. While I was quickly adapting to my new environment, I remained nervous and tried to behave appropriately. The decision to jump on the couch seemed critical at the time, and I was worried about making an error and disappointing Dad and his roommate.

Suddenly, the front door flew open, and a petite woman with flowing hair and a sunny smile breezed into the room. She spoke warmly and approached me slowly with one hand extended for my inspection. While I'm generally timid around strangers, I immediately relaxed and eagerly sniffed her palm. She smelled like fresh coffee and of something sweet that she ate on the way here, leaving sugar on her fingertips. I hesitantly licked her hand, savoring the flavor of her recent snack. She cooed happily and began gently stroking my back, lulling me into a meditative state.

My sister barreled over to investigate our visitor and began to prance about as the woman attempted to pet her. Sara sniffed her from the tips of her fingers to the laces of her shoes, circling to assess her from all angles. Sara then drenched the woman's palm with her slobbery tongue, indicating her approval.

Dad came out of the bedroom, embraced the woman, and stared lovingly into her eyes before turning back to Sara and me. He pointed at each of us, stated our names in turn, and the woman repeated them softly. My name had never sounded so sweet, and I had a good feeling about her. She had access to our home, which meant that she was on the trusted visitor's list. I was eager to impress her so she would return often to scratch my back.

The woman knelt and continued to pet us while softly repeating our names. I slid closer to her and sat quietly, stealing glances at her before returning my gaze to the floor. I didn't want to stare and preferred to avert my eyes to avoid seeming aggressive or intrusive. As I relaxed, my head began to droop, and I eventually lay down. I exhaled deeply and rested my chin on my paws, feeling deeply loved. The woman continued to shower me with attention, obviously wanting to make my acquaintance and gain my trust, which is not a difficult task because I am drawn to anyone who offers back rubs and whispers kind words.

She and Dad took a seat at the kitchen table and began to chat. I observed the interaction from my position on the floor, temporarily satisfied by the prolonged back scratch. However, if they walked in my direction, I would wag my tail excitedly, smile warmly, and raise my eyebrows for maximum cuteness. This is a tried-and-tested way of obtaining a hug and a head pat. I never pass up an opportunity to snuggle.

I heard our names repeated multiple times during their conversation and was thrilled that they were discussing us. I didn't understand what they were saying, but it sounded enthusiastic, and I took that as a positive sign. They periodically glanced over at us and smiled, which was a sure sign that they were happy with me.

Sara lay quietly by my side and drifted off to sleep. How could she sleep when there was an exciting visitor in the house? She was breathing heavily with her stinky breath aimed in my direction. I was used to this bad habit by now, but she could benefit from one of those green dental bones, which I've heard are healthy for our teeth. I wondered if I might find any stowed away in hiding spots around the room. I'd have to put my nose to the test later and investigate the situation. The thought made my tail wag, and I envisioned uncovering a treasure trove of assorted treats in an open bag that I could easily access. This is a recurring dream, and I'm hopeful that it will come true.

Within minutes, Dad and the woman wandered over to the couch and made themselves comfortable. My eyes tracked them as they crossed the room, and I studied the pleasing contours of the woman's face, trying to memorize every curve. When she called me over, I rose to my paws and trotted to her side. She rewarded me with a soft kiss on the top of my head and a soothing word. The woman said my name again, and I felt gooey inside because she was thoroughly smitten with me.

Feeling shy again, I stood quietly, enjoying the attention and the sound of her voice as she spoke to Dad. I moved closer until my head was resting on her lap, and I worried that she would move aside or push me away, but instead, she welcomed my approach and hugged me gently. I felt a surge of sheer joy, and my tail began to wag involuntarily. I had won her over and hoped that she would stay forever.

I gazed around at my new home, suddenly possessive of the space. While I wouldn't say that it was mine yet, that was the plan, and I would gladly defend the apartment from any intruders. I was willing to work hard to convince Dad and the kind woman that I was loyal, well-behaved, and adorable. Hopefully, they'd decide that I deserved to be cuddled and spoiled. I had heard of households where dogs were treated as valued members of the family and given every luxury in life, but until this moment, I wasn't sure if they existed. I already loved this place and was grateful that Dad had picked me. I'm sure many other dogs were competing for his affection, but he selected my sister and me from the crowd and seemed intent on making our lives pleasant and comfortable. I would be eternally grateful to him for opening his home and heart, and I would do my best to show my appreciation.

## The Bark Diaries

When the sweet lady left the next day, I was discouraged and unsure if she intended to return. However, I didn't have to wait long, and we soon established a pattern of her spending several nights with us each week. Those were always my favorite days, and while I loved Dad with all my heart, no one could compete with my adopted Mom.

Leslie Popp

*Rachel*

## Boundaries

I struggle more with physical boundaries than emotional or psychological ones. While changes in flooring and doorways may not be intimidating to you, they're a major impediment for me. This fear began with some negative incidents in my first home when I was a puppy. I've never been able to overcome it, nor do I like thinking about it. My new family is everything I've always dreamed of, and I try to live in the moment and focus on the positive things.

As I'm lounging on the couch, I can hear Mom shuffling around in the bedroom and getting ready for the day. I have sensitive ears and make a point of monitoring her movements, even when she thinks I'm not paying attention. My top priority is protecting and caring for my family, and I'm always ready to assist Mom whenever she needs my help. Even if I can't solve the problem, Mom always looks happy to see me, which makes my heart soar and my tail wag uncontrollably. Our bond grows stronger by the day despite having recently met. I'm already quite attached to her, and I think the feeling is mutual.

# The Bark Diaries

There's a loud clatter, and I immediately leap to my feet in alarm, hop off the couch, and trot to the bedroom door to investigate. I hope Mom hasn't fallen and hurt herself because I haven't been trained in first aid and don't have a background in medicine, which hinders my ability to treat her.

Perhaps I could learn more about this field, but I despise going to the vet and prefer to avoid doctors. You can't trust people in long white coats who work in sanitized facilities perfumed with the scents of other animals. While they seem friendly, someone inevitably pokes me with a needle when my back is turned, which is not acceptable in my opinion. You should never ambush anyone like that and always ask permission before jabbing them with a sharp object. I'd like to see how they'd react if treated the same way. I'm certain it wouldn't go well, but then they'd finally understand why I'm so nervous in their office.

I reach the bedroom doorway and look down at the floor, suddenly frozen at the threshold. Stepping through the doorway seems daunting, and my paws are glued to the spot. I gaze into the room and see Mom pulling on a stretchy shirt, apparently unharmed and unfazed by the scary noise. I heave a sigh of relief and feel the tension in my muscles ease. I'm in charge of her safety, and I take that responsibility seriously. I won't let anything happen to my family while I'm on guard duty.

Concluding that there's no immediate threat, I return to puzzling over the tricky doorway situation. I pace back and forth, debating whether it's safe to cross from the living room into the bedroom. The doorway seems intimidating and ominous, and there was a time in my life when I wasn't permitted to roam the house. That's in the past now, but the memory remains and gives me pause at every change of flooring or division of space within the house. Gazing into the room again, I lift one paw, trying to muster my courage and conquer my fear. However, I can't bring myself to take the crucial step. I remain perfectly still, contemplating the issue and growing increasingly desperate.

Mom finds me standing motionless and takes action to resolve the predicament. She's familiar with my challenges and always encourages me to be brave. As much as I appreciate her support, I wish that I was bolder and able to wander through rooms at my leisure, but my skittish nature hinders this kind of free-spirited behavior. Mom crouches, extends her arms toward me, and smiles warmly. She encourages me to run to her for a hug and a back rub.

I wag my tail fiercely, perk up my ears, and smile, displaying my pink tongue. This expression has a delightful effect on humans, who find it endearing and impossible not to provide some affection. It's also useful when begging for treats, because who could resist this expression?

Mom calls my name and waves, which piques my interest and causes me to pace frantically. If there were no doorways in the apartment, then I could prance about freely, following Mom and Dad from one area to the next with reckless disregard for non-existent thresholds. I desperately want to rush to her. I appreciate the welcoming gesture and want to reciprocate by resting my head on her leg and gently licking her hand, but that's difficult to do from this distance, and she seems content to remain seated on the floor.

## The Bark Diaries

I close my eyes, take a deep breath, and again lift one paw. Telling myself to be strong, I attempt to place it down on the opposite side of the doorway. Before it touches the floor, a wave of anxiety washes over me, and I retreat a step to regroup.

Mom crawls forward, reaches out, and softly pats my head. I gaze into her big brown eyes as she gently tugs my collar and guides me into the room. I'm tense while crossing the threshold but immediately relax when nothing life-threatening happens.

This is a delightful space, and suddenly, I can't remember why it was so intimidating. Sunlight is streaming through the windows, and everything looks soft and cozy. There are many new smells to investigate, and I'm keenly aware that someone was eating snacks in bed last night. I wonder if there are any stray crumbs on the floor that need to be eaten. I'm always available to help clean up spilled food; in fact, it's one of my special skills.

I walk around the room, sniffing everything in sight and wishing I was taller to fully explore the bed and dresser. I have no idea if there is food on top of them that requires my attention, but I suppose some mysteries will remain unsolved.

I plunge my nose into Mom's shoe and catch a whiff of sweaty feet, grime, and a piece of gum clinging to the bottom. These shoes have traveled the world and emit the smells to prove it. I then detect an unfamiliar animal scent coming from the overnight bag that she always carries. A few pieces of orange fur cling to the fabric, and I wonder what creature left its mark on her belongings. This mystery puzzles me, and for a moment, I worry there's competition for her affection.

As I'm debating this problem, Mom kneels beside me and rubs my back. I whirl around, delighted to see her smiling face and pleased that it's at head level. Slowly, I lean forward, giving her ample time to pull away if she's uncomfortable with the close proximity. She holds her position and beams at me. I hesitantly close the distance and lick her cheek. I'm always nervous about kissing her and invading her personal space, so I make a point of approaching slowly to avoid startling her. She giggles and wraps her arms around me in a warm embrace. My tail wags, knocking against the dresser with a rhythmic thumping sound. I feel safe with her, and for a moment, my fears seem like distant memories.

We sit on the ground, enjoying each other's company and sharing a peaceful moment. Then Mom rises to her feet and walks softly out of the room. I follow her closely but come to an abrupt halt at the doorway and gaze into the living room. I was on the couch beside my sleeping sister only minutes ago, but now the threshold keeps me trapped in the bedroom. I stare down at the invisible divide, sighing heavily as my heart begins to sink. Mom, my brave and fearless protector, appears by my side and leads me across the boundary into the living room. I relax and lick her hand, feeling grateful for the prompt assistance. It has been an eventful day, and I've taken a small step toward becoming a bold explorer. There's a long way to go, but I'll eventually have grand adventures and race from room to room without hesitation. For now, I still need Mom's guidance and reassurance.

Mom tousles my fur, kisses the top of my head, and wanders away. Exhausted from facing my fears, I hop onto the couch, turn in a circle three times, then once more for good measure, and curl into a tight ball. I rest my head on my paws and think about spaces without doorways and with uniform flooring. There would be little privacy, but I prefer to be by Mom's side, so that wouldn't be an issue. Maybe someday we'll knock down these walls and live in one large open space. One can only dream!

Leslie Popp

## *Sara*

## A Beginner's Guide to Demanding Back Rubs

The prospect of receiving back rubs and head scratches motivates me, and I'm always on the lookout for friendly people willing to pet me. Over the years, I've honed this valuable skill and now consider myself to be an expert in my field. By now, I should have been offered an honorary degree or a medal for my groundbreaking research on human behavior and assessing the likelihood of receiving pets in any scenario. My findings would be beneficial for dogs worldwide. I've spent many afternoons thinking about how to spread the news and share my insights. I don't have a solution yet, but I'll devise a clever strategy to communicate with dogs across the city and around the world.

I have scholarly thoughts about how to acquire food and coax friendly people into affectionately stroking my shaggy fur. When I'm asleep, I dream of belly rubs. You might call it an obsession, but I consider my interest in back scratches to be an intellectual pursuit. Given my limited responsibilities around the house, I have plenty of time during the day to conduct my research.

For example, if someone is sitting or lying on the couch watching TV, then the likelihood of head scratches is high, especially if their hands are idle. In this situation, you should approach them directly and rest your chin on their knee or their stomach. This triggers an automatic signal to their brain that tells them to say "awww" and begin rhythmically running their hand from the top of your head down your back. Then you simply stand still and give them a wide-eyed gaze to express your gratitude. I use this method regularly and guarantee results when it's applied correctly.

If your human is playing on their phone while watching TV, then you should alter your tactics. Humans are often engrossed in these devices, rendering them oblivious to their surroundings, so you must be more aggressive. I wonder why they attempt to use the TV and phone simultaneously because they can't pay attention to two devices at once. When both screens are chattering loudly, it's impossible to follow the conversations. My limited vocabulary is also an issue.

Anyway, if your human is holding their phone, then you should approach them with confidence, pant heavily in their face, and nuzzle their hands so they're forced to abandon the device. If you can remove the pesky machine from their grasp, that's even better. They're very protective of their phones and become anxious when they strike hard surfaces. I strongly dislike phones because they distract humans from their loving animals and are an unnecessary part of life. I've never needed a phone, which is proof that they're useless devices. But since phones are everywhere and won't go away in my lifetime, we must learn to deal with their challenges.

Anyway, the next scenario is when your human's friends come to visit and stand around chatting about insignificant issues. You should carefully observe the group to select an initial target. Some humans wave their hands when they talk, which is entertaining but not ideal for petting purposes. Look for someone who has at least one hand hanging loosely by their side.

Once a target is selected, stroll over and position the top of your head against their hand so they can easily open and close their fingers to scratch your head. This simplifies the process and makes your intentions known. Research shows that they will immediately pet you. To thank them, wag your tail enthusiastically and lean against their leg for an additional neck massage. This is the ideal and most likely outcome.

If the person you targeted doesn't respond as expected, then they're probably not an animal lover. You should redirect your attention to the rest of the group and either select another human or systematically approach each individual and press your head against their hand. You can sniff their pants and lick their fingers for maximum effect. Eventually, you'll find an obliging friend and can remain close by their side for the rest of the event.

Let's think through a scenario where you're out for a walk. Are you allowed to approach strangers? This is an important question because you don't want to anger your human by prancing up to an unfamiliar person and requesting attention. Some dogs struggle when meeting new acquaintances; if this describes your personality, skip this section of the lesson.

When you're out for an afternoon stroll on a beautiful day and you see a friendly-looking human walking toward you, here's what my research suggests you should do. First, lift the corners of your lips to mimic a human smile, let your mouth hang open so your tongue sticks out, and raise your eyebrows. This is a welcoming expression that invites the person to approach you. Then block their path on the sidewalk so a head-on collision is inevitable. This forces the person to stop and creates a golden opportunity to lick their hand, arm, leg, or wherever you can reach. Wait patiently to see if they react positively to this display of affection. If they're excited to meet you, then wag your tail in the air like you just don't care and sit at their feet for a free massage.

This is how new friends are made and how you establish a back rub network. If that individual lives in the neighborhood, then the likelihood of receiving massages on future walks is high. Once you've formed a bond, they'll always be excited to see you and scratch behind your ears or rub the itchy spot on your side. If you cultivate friendships in your neighborhood, you're more likely to receive frequent attention.

Now, you might be wondering what to do if you encounter a dog-friendly human that has a four-legged companion. This is a highly complex situation that must be handled with extreme care and consideration.

First, evaluate the intentions of the fluffy companion to determine if the dog seems interested in meeting you and your human or if it is standoffish and protective of its person.

If it's curious, slowly lead your human in that direction to see how the other dog reacts. If it begins to show any defensive signs, quickly redirect and wander away, leaving the dog and its owner in peace. There's no reason to cause a scene, and other opportunities for attention will emerge on future walks. If the dog and its human welcome your approach, then cautiously proceed for an introduction.

Approach the dog head-on and allow it to sniff you, signaling that you mean no harm. If things are going well, then you can lean in for a butt sniff to be polite. Once the other dog determines that you're not aggressive and are an acceptable addition to its afternoon outing, you can appeal to its human for a back rub. Given this person is already an animal lover, you can be confident that they'll greet you with head pats and butt scratches. Don't forget to wag your tail and present them with the smile we previously discussed. Challenging their dog for attention is not advised, but instead insert yourself into their walk as a best friend and not a competitor.

If you follow these guidelines, you'll be sure to receive affection and cultivate a valuable network of back scratchers. I'm available to answer any questions or analyze additional situations. Good luck, and I hope these rules are as effective for you as they are for me.

## Rachel

### Kibble vs. Pizza

There's nothing better than a bowl of fresh kibble that smells like sweet potato, brown rice, and a hint of apple. I am a vegan dog, and Dad always chooses the highest quality food to ensure that I have enough vitamins and minerals to stay strong and healthy. Just look at my shiny coat!

My nose is highly sensitive and acutely focused on my bowl, which I consider sacred territory. I always scarf down my normal kibble and feel elated whenever Dad walks toward the food bag, but I'll eat just about anything. Whatever is placed in my bowl is considered edible and up for grabs. If you blink, I'll make it disappear. You could call me a kibble magician with a talent for making food vanish.

When anyone nears my dish, my eyes lock onto their movements in case they leave a tasty morsel behind and forget to tell me. I'm prepared to make a mad dash for the bowl at the first hint of a snack, ensuring that I arrive before my sister lopes over and gobbles it up. She's bigger than me, but her disabled leg slows her down. However, that doesn't stop her from being pushy during mealtimes, and she never hesitates to claim any delicacies. Sara is more boisterous by nature and demands first dibs on our bowls.

There are two food bowls to choose from, but Sara and I share everything. We often eat from the same bowl, ignoring the second dish and knocking our heads together as we swap spit while hovering over the kibble and crunching loudly in unison. Sometimes I start with one bowl, Sara joins in, then I retreat to the second bowl, and she quickly follows. We have a system worked out, but I'll admit that occasionally I would appreciate some personal space to inhale my food in peace. It's a race to see who can swallow more barely chewed kibble before the bowls grow barren and empty.

Empty food bowls are the worst. There's nothing more depressing than seeing the bottom of the bowl and realizing that I have no idea how long it'll be until lunch. It has nothing to do with how hungry I feel. Eating is a delightful treat for the soul and stomach. Lunch is always fleeting because when my meal is served, I devour it at an impressive rate and am left in my current predicament, staring at an empty bowl and wondering who ate all my food. Did I do that? The dish was full only moments ago, and I couldn't possibly have eaten so quickly, but I must have.

I look over at my sister, who is lapping up the remnants from the second bowl and collecting crumbs on her nose. I consider squeezing in and retrieving the scraps, but she's too busy licking the bottom of that dish until it shines. We do an outstanding job at scrubbing our dishes and removing any leftover food. Dad washes his bowls in the sink with water, but we would happily lick them clean. I don't mind doing my share of the chores, but he has never asked me to perform this duty. Nevertheless, I'm always prepared and ready to intervene, and you will never hear me complaining about tidying up after meals. No ma'am, this dog is ready to report for dishwasher duty, and you won't have to pay me or ask twice. I would undoubtedly be the ideal candidate for the job, and I hope Dad notices how well I clean my bowl.

He often leaves plates covered with crumbs or half-eaten meals lying around the apartment. The low coffee table in the living room is one of his favorite lunch spots, and if I were so inclined, I could easily swoop in and devour the food before he realized what had happened. However, I would never do something like that because it's not my food, and I want Dad to remain big and strong and live a long life with Sara and me. It would be rude to take someone else's food without their permission. He doesn't steal my kibble, and I want to return the favor.

If Dad was willing to share his lunch with me, he would offer a morsel from the palm of his hand, and I would gladly accept it. The thought makes my mouth water, so I wander over to see what's on his plate today. I stay close to him during meals in case he requires assistance finishing his food. I enjoy his company and prefer to be by his side.

I smell cheese, bread, tomato, and an array of pungent seasonings. Yes, it's pizza day! I assume a sentry position beside the coffee table, staring intently at the food, knowing that I could easily snatch a piece and flee. I could take a few bites before Dad wrestles it away, but as I said before, it's not my food, and I know better.

## Leslie Popp

Dad glances at me and extends his hand. I leap to my feet and race over to see if it contains food. His palm is empty, but he gives me a hearty back scratch, and I excitedly wag my tail and wiggle my butt for maximum effect. My mouth hangs open, and my tongue lolls out as I lovingly stare at him. His breath smells like cheese, and I consider licking his face to see if he tastes like pizza, too.

He returns to his meal, quickly finishing one greasy slice before starting another. I sit next to him with my head resting on his knee, hoping that when something drops on the ground, it will be meant for me. Any food that falls to the floor is automatically mine, which is my favorite house rule. I don't understand why humans won't eat food that has fallen on the floor. It's the same food that they were devouring from their plate seconds ago. Somehow, a transformation occurs once it hits the floor, and they deem it unworthy of returning to their plates. I shouldn't complain because I consider floor food to be superior anyway. Maybe my palate is less refined, but if it tastes good and is free, I'm on board. Throw it all on the floor!

I'm not feeling lucky today as Dad finishes his last piece of pizza without dropping a single crumb. I sigh heavily, wishing that he would lose his grip on the fragrant slice and let it plummet to the hardwood floor. There's a routine we follow every time he drops food, and it goes something like this. He appears shocked at his clumsy error, glances over at me, and points to the food on the ground, as though I haven't already spotted it. I enthusiastically report for cleanup duty. There's no food too sticky, chewy, or liquidy for me to

## The Bark Diaries

thoroughly scrub from our floors. Everything will be shiny and sanitized when I'm done.

Dad finishes chewing, wipes his mouth with a napkin, and walks into the kitchen, leaving the pizza unattended. Now I have a serious dilemma. I'm a good dog, and a good dog doesn't take people's food. However, perhaps Dad has discarded this food, and I wouldn't want it to go to waste.

I stare at the pizza, my mouth watering at the sight of the cheese and toasted bread. I can almost taste it, and the aroma is overwhelming. Perhaps I could take a tiny nibble or lick the cheese and savor the greasy texture in my mouth. No, no, no, Dad would certainly notice and suspect me because I'm the only one around to blame. I don't want to upset him, so I try to banish the idea from my mind and focus on other things like the kibble I plan to inhale from my bowl at my next meal. The thought of eating the same old dog food makes my craving for pizza even harder to resist. I'm obsessed with this cheesy delight.

Dad returns with his phone and collapses onto the couch, staring at his phone, becoming engrossed in a noisy video. I step toward the coffee table and pause to wait for Dad's reaction, but he doesn't look up and continues smiling at the device. I take another step, keeping my head low and my eyes trained on the ground, trying to convey that I'm an obedient pup who will respond to any of his commands. If he gives me the "no" command, then that means no, and if he says "sit," then I'll sit, but if he says nothing, then the situation is open to interpretation.

I inch forward and glance over at Dad with anticipation. Perhaps he hasn't noticed my slow progression, but I choose to assume that he has no further use for the pizza and has left it on the table for me to enjoy. There's more than enough to share, and he must know how delicious it smells. This thought puts me at ease because surely he can relate to the allure of the scent that's dominating the room. You can't ignore the aroma of melted cheese on fresh bread.

I'm now hovering at the edge of the table, barely able to contain my excitement. I linger for a moment, giving him the opportunity to whisk the pizza away or provide further instruction, which I would obediently follow. However, the long seconds tick by, and I receive no feedback, which means that I'm in the clear. The food is mine!

Slowly, I lean forward, inhale the delightful aroma, clamp my teeth around a slice of pizza, and drag it onto the floor. I quickly tear it into pieces and swallow them whole, despite my intention to thoroughly chew my food. I usually like to savor the flavor, but I'm so excited and can't stop myself from devouring the pizza at record speed.

Suddenly, the delicious treat is snatched away, and I'm stunned to see Dad clutching the remnants of my pilfered slice in his hand. It's a gooey pile of cheese, sauce, and bread. Giving him a guilty look, I sniff his hand, hoping that he'll return the remaining pieces. He holds the scraps out of my reach and firmly tells me no.

I lower my head and stare at the ground, realizing that the food wasn't meant for me. Perhaps he didn't react to my approach because he believed that I would never interfere with his lunch spread. I hope that I haven't betrayed his trust. The pizza was out in the open, and I couldn't stop myself from indulging, even knowing that it was probably wrong.

## The Bark Diaries

Oh, why did I do it? A good dog doesn't steal food from the table.

Then I notice a bit of sauce and grease on the ground by my feet and quickly lick the floor clean because it's tasty, and I don't want Dad to see that I've made a mess. Once the situation has been remedied, there's only a wet mark left to denote the spot. I take a moment to reflect on the situation.

I worry that Dad is mad at me, but then he wanders over and tousles the fur on the top of my head. I gaze up at him with wide eyes, trying to convey that I never meant to break the rules and have nothing but the utmost respect for his personal property. If we can pretend that this didn't happen, I promise not to do it again.

I sit quietly at his feet, staring down at the ground and feeling ashamed of myself. He understands that I'm apologetic and kneels to give me a gentle hug, which does wonders to reassure me of his love and affection. I know how much he cares for me, but my anxiety makes me wonder whether every minor infraction causes irreparable damage to our relationship.

Dad strokes my fur and softly whispers my name, which has never sounded so sweet. My ears perk up, and my tail wags gently. We sit this way for several minutes, enjoying each other's company. I don't need pizza to be happy, only loving moments when nothing else in the world matters. I adore Dad, and I'm his special girl.

He pats my side and rises to his feet, and I lick my lips, removing the last traces of grease from my fur. Maybe next time he'll drop a slice on the ground, and the situation will be simpler. I lie down, and drift off into a peaceful slumber, dreaming about floor food.

## Rachel

### The Thing About Toys

If you've never seen a tennis ball before, please allow me to explain. They are greenish-yellow balls that bounce energetically and roll swiftly across the floor with just a gentle push. They are perfectly round, with unfamiliar black marks scrawled across their surface. Humans enjoy playing with tennis balls, and there's always one wedged under the TV stand, resting in the corner, or positioned in the center of the table where it can be admired by all.

I'm sprawled out on the floor in front of Mom with my head tilted to one side, watching her with interest. She looks excited, and her enthusiasm is contagious because there's nothing I love more than spending long afternoons by her side. She speaks animatedly, occasionally patting the top of my head.

Mom picks up the ball from the table and holds it out for me to examine. I lean forward and give it a thorough sniff, taking in the scent of her hand, rubber, and dirt, which I can tell originated from the sidewalk outside.

## Leslie Popp

"Wow, this is an exceptional tennis ball! It's brightly colored and goes nicely with my fur," I think, enjoying the vibrant hue that livens up the room.

"Good girl," Mom replies, scratching my head.

I am such a good girl! Wagging my tail with excitement, I look up at her, wondering what I did to deserve her praise. It doesn't really matter, and I'm just glad that she called me a good girl because that's what all dogs aspire to be. Our ultimate goal and grandest achievement in life is to be awarded the title of Good Dog. I've worked hard to maintain my reputation, and my effort is paying off.

Mom bounces the ball, which makes a hollow sound on impact, and it rebounds into her hand. I watch as she repeats this several times, wondering what she's doing. Maybe she's testing the ball's aerodynamic properties or the strength of the hardwood floor. Whatever the reason, it makes her happy, and that's all that matters. She glances over, and I open my mouth in a wide smile, thinking that we should make the most of this amusing activity since my afternoon is completely free.

Mom places the ball on the ground and gently rolls it in my direction. I watch as it approaches, holding completely still as it travels between my paws and comes to rest against my chest. I sniff it again, then glance back at Mom, who is watching me closely, as though expecting me to respond. I stare at her, content to let the ball rest against my fur. I'll diligently guard her toy and keep it safe between my paws. This seems like an important job, and I will give it my full attention.

She points to the ball, but I don't see anything of interest. We repeat this process several times, and I begin to wonder if I'm missing something. Does she want the ball back? I wonder what I'm expected to do with it now. Are we admiring the spherical qualities that allow it to roll?

I ponder the situation, feeling certain that I'm overlooking a key element in this interaction. Perhaps there's a way to open the ball and reveal a secret treat. Carefully, I inspect it, checking for holes, buttons, or seams that would suggest it could be broken apart or popped open, but nothing stands out to me, and I'm back where I started.

Mom picks up the ball and retreats a few feet before rolling it back to me. It travels between my paws and bumps lightly against my chest once again. I am pleased to hold onto it for her, but she seems to expect more from me. I tilt my head, now thoroughly confused by the situation. I've encountered tennis balls many times, yet I still haven't figured out their purpose. I always watch them closely to ensure they don't do anything suspicious or try to wander away. This one seems harmless and hasn't attempted to escape.

Mom scoops up the ball and holds it in front of my nose, and I tilt my head in uncertainty. Then she rolls the ball across the room where it comes to rest against the wall. She looks at me, then at the ball, then back at me, and finally points to it, as if I didn't notice. She retrieves the ball, tosses it gently, waits for me to respond, and then goes to fetch it herself.

I'm beginning to understand the game. Mom enjoys chasing the ball, and I'll gladly be her cheerleader. The yellow toy flies straight and true and bounces enthusiastically when it hits the floor. Tennis balls are a wonderful invention, and Mom is getting plenty of exercise chasing this one around. I sigh and rest my head on my paws, content to spend the afternoon lounging with Mom.

"If there's any way I can help, just let me know," I say, raising my eyebrows and glancing up at her. "It seems like you've got this activity under control, and I don't want to interrupt your game."

She rubs my head and speaks softly, lulling me into a meditative state. I love spending time with Mom and supervising her activities. This exercise is an excellent workout for her, given she has to run back and forth to retrieve the ball after throwing it. I'm not sure why she doesn't just hold onto it, but who am I to judge humans for their games? She appears to enjoy the sport, but it's a simple activity, and I worry that she'll grow bored. I never tire of watching the ball roll around and delight in the hollow thump it makes with every bounce. I may never understand humans, but I've finally mastered this game.

## *Sara*

## The Art of Shedding

If there's one thing that I excel at in life, it's shedding. My fur must grow at super speed because my golden hairs fly off when I shake and coat every surface in the house. I don't know exactly how I do it, but it's a natural talent. When I lose one piece, another must spring up to replace it because my soft coat remains thick and fluffy.

I can create a fur tornado by planting my paws firmly on the floor, shaking aggressively, and letting the fur fly. It's something to behold if you've never witnessed the phenomenon. All Golden Retrievers have this power, and I'm happy to demonstrate it if you're interested.

Rachel, on the other hand, doesn't share my shedding power, and her shorter coat clings to her. It's a shame because if we both had my ability, then we could create soft fur mats to lie on and possibly a matching coat for Mom. It would be ideal if she had a full coat of fur, too.

Every few days, fur tumbleweeds accumulate around the apartment and blow across the floor with the slightest breeze when a fan is turned on or a window opened. I like watching the furballs drift around, but Mom views them as a sign to roll out the dreaded vacuum. We're frequently terrorized by the roaring machine that gobbles up my lovely fur and combs the area for any stray hairs that try to flee in its wake. The vacuum inhales everything, except the fur that covers the couch, which must be removed by hand.

I'll admit that my fluffy coat can be hot in the summer because dogs can't change their fur seasonally the way humans adjust their clothing. We would look silly without our natural fur, and I've never seen myself without it. However, we attempt to rid ourselves of excess hair to provide some relief from the heat. When the weather begins to turn, my shedding goes into overdrive. Mom always says that I'm a very efficient shedder, and just when she thinks that I can't get any better at it, summer rolls around again, and I prove her wrong.

My thick coat presents some challenges. For instance, if I spill food on my paw and try to lick it off, I inevitably end up with a mouthful of hair. It interferes with the flavor of the food and sticks to my tongue, but the inconvenience is worth it to savor that stray crumb. I would never want to waste food, and kibble is sacred in this house.

Baths are also a tricky situation, and I prefer to avoid them, but Mom and Dad insist that they're necessary. I'm periodically forced to endure the tiresome process of being soaped up and rinsed off, leaving my fluffy fur waterlogged and dripping everywhere. Imagine a fur bomb going off in the bathtub, with clumps of my hair clogging the drain. Bathing is a messy business, and it takes hours to dry the layers of soft down beneath my wiry outer coat. I always smell after a bath, and the odd scent lingers for days. It's as though I need a bath after my bath to rid myself of the shampoo aroma. How am I supposed to mark my territory if my fur no longer carries my distinctive scent?

Mom has experimented with different brushes on my long tresses, and we've finally settled on a wide comb with small metal teeth. She believes that periodic brushing will help with the constant shedding, but she's wrong. It doesn't matter how much she brushes me; I'll always have more fur in reserve to build those wonderful tumbleweeds, even if it takes an extra day or two.

When I'm sprawled on the floor, Mom will sit next to me and run that special brush from the top of my head down to my tail, removing loose fur along the way. After a few passes, the teeth are full of golden hair, and Mom has to pause and remove the blockage. The short bristles tickle my skin and occasionally snag on a knot that we either have to snip off or gently detangle. I tend to squirm during this part. As Mom brushes my side, the pile of fur grows larger, and no matter how much she brushes, the bristles always come away clutching more hair. She can only brush one side of me at a time because I refuse to roll over, so Mom has to remember which side she recently brushed and patiently wait for me to reposition myself to access the other side. This is an amusing game, and I enjoy her undivided attention.

Mom then collects the pile of fur and disposes of it in the large trash can. I think she should save that fur and stuff the cushions with it or keep some in her pockets so she smells like me. This would let other dogs know that she already has a canine companion. The fur could also serve as a loving reminder of me when we're not together, and I'm sure it would put a smile on her face. It seems a shame to throw away that lovely ball of fur, even though I'll generate more by tomorrow.

Let's talk about my paws. They're a bit unconventional because I have very hairy toes. The layer of fuzz protects my feet from the cold, but I struggle to grip the slick hardwood floors. I occasionally slide awkwardly around the living room but usually regain my balance before anyone witnesses the humiliating incident.

The shaggy fur conceals my nails, which I try to keep hidden from Mom. She insists on trimming them on a regular basis, but I strongly object. I don't mind when they grow long and clack against the floor, announcing my presence as I stroll into a room. Mom waits until I'm napping, then sneaks up quietly, and snips off the ends of my nails. After one or two clips, I wake up and put a stop to the nonsense, pulling away and resting my head on my paws so she can't access them. Go away; there's nothing to see here.

It's a slow process, but Mom strategically waits for me to doze off again before creeping up and clipping another nail or two until she has shortened all of them. I make this difficult by switching sides, forcing her to remember which ones she previously trimmed. I believe that my fear is warranted. Rachel shakes during the nail clipping process and tucks all four paws beneath her to elude the dreaded clippers. Mom is determined and tells us that it's for our own good. I trust her, but I would still prefer to skip this part of the grooming process.

# The Bark Diaries

I love Mom, but she has strange ideas about self-care that make little sense to me. My shedding is inevitable, and no amount of brushing will stop my golden hairs from scattering around the house and producing those corner tumbleweeds. My nails are continuously growing, and they don't bother me in the slightest. I dislike cutting them more than letting them grow to their natural length and click against the floor. My vote would be that we continue the brushing, given it provides a nice bonding time for Mom and me, but scrap the nail treatments, which are stressful for everyone.

I wander over to my water bowl, leaving a trail of fur in my wake, which will let Mom know where I've gone. As I lower my head to take a cool drink, my eyes spot something odd on the floor. I turn my attention to the discovery and bend down to investigate. My eyes grow wide, and my mouth falls open in surprise.

Coiled on the floor is a long brown hair that doesn't belong to Rachel or me. It bears Mom's scent and must have come from her. The color matches her dark hair, which reaches halfway down her back and sways gracefully when she walks. It is truly incredible. Mom is shedding! We should probably start brushing her.

Leslie Popp

*Rachel*

## Neighborhood Patrol

I love strolling around the neighborhood on sunny afternoons, pausing to sniff every light pole and pee in the manicured flower bed on the corner. There's no better feeling than the fresh air on your nose, the breeze gently ruffling the fur on your cheeks, and the bird songs drifting through the warm air. I live for these refreshing walks.

As a New York City pup, I've become accustomed to the constant traffic, the smell of exotic spices from nearby restaurants, the voices of strangers that power walk up and down the street and chatter away at all hours, and the resident dogs. I live on a comparatively quiet street lined with tall trees and elegant brick buildings. The river is just steps away, and I can smell the water from our front stoop.

It's a crisp spring day, and Mom and I are on our morning patrol. She's an early riser and always accompanies Sara and I on the first stroll. Sara is still groggy from her deep slumber, but I'm perky and curious to see if there are any other dogs about.

# The Bark Diaries

I lead Mom down the street, ensuring that she has a tight hold on my leash, which tethers us together and keeps her from wandering away. I don't know how strong her nose or sense of direction are, but if she becomes disoriented from the activity and commotion on the street, then I can always lead her home. The leash makes me feel secure with the knowledge that she's close by.

Admittedly, the leash also prevents me from trotting into the street, which is useful because I'm terrible at checking for cars before crossing. I know I should be more careful, but I get so excited that I forget to look both ways before stepping off the curb. It's a good thing that Mom is alert and attentive because she's in charge of watching for moving vehicles and safely guiding us across the road. We have an excellent system in place, and the leash is a valuable tool that benefits us both.

"This way!" I call, making a beeline toward the nearest light pole. "I need to check who else has been out this morning."

Sara hops along beside me, using her three good legs to propel her forward and the disabled leg to stabilize her movements. She is never bothered by her disability and can romp around quite vigorously when she puts her mind to it. She has always been a happy, optimistic dog that walks on sunshine. I admire her attitude and confidence because she doesn't let her unsteady gait hold her back. She is just excited to be alive and intent on exploring the world.

We stop at the light pole and vigorously sniff the base, rotating together in a coordinated dance and thoroughly assessing the smells that waft up our noses. Yep, all the regulars have been here this morning and left their unique scents behind. Humans use mailboxes and phones to communicate with each other, and we use light poles. I squat and scatter my scent in the area, and Sara quickly follows my lead. We stare at each other for a moment, pleased that the next canine to wander by will know that we've commenced our morning patrol.

I prefer to stick to our normal haunts and trot a specific route, which we've officially claimed as our territory but is actually shared with other four-legged residents. Given we live in New York City, it would be impossible to stake an exclusive claim to any piece of sidewalk. That being said, I still periodically mark light poles, trash cans, flower beds, and the occasional tree to let other dogs know that we're locals, not tourists, and expect to be shown respect.

I'm not very social, and while I'm generally a docile pup that is not aggressive toward humans, my guard is always up around other dogs. Don't get me wrong, I enjoy a good butt sniff to become better acquainted with the regulars on our walks, but I want it to be on my terms. I'm protective of my sister because of her unwieldy gait, which sometimes unsettles dogs that are unfamiliar with her condition. They are often skeptical and approach her out of curiosity. My instinct is to immediately intervene and force them to retreat, heading off any issues and ensuring that Sara is safe.

Sara on the other hand is unfazed by new acquaintances and maintains her welcoming disposition. She's curious by nature and happily greets unfamiliar people and animals, automatically assuming that they're friendly and willing to offer treats and back scratches. I crave snacks as much as the next dog, but my protective instinct is strong, and I approach every situation with caution. This sometimes results in me barking at another pooch out of fear.

We continue our circuit, and I force us to stop at every dog mailbox, if you will, to analyze the coded messages and add my own to the mix. Mom doesn't understand the importance of this communication system and attempts to pass the next light pole without pausing.

"Wait," I whine. "We can't skip one and break the pattern."

"Come on, Rachel," she calls, beckoning me forward. "We have to do some actual walking or we'll never make it around the block."

I oblige since I've successfully marked the last five poles, and the tank is now empty. However, when we repeat this route midday, I'll pick up where I left off.

I pause in front of the pizza place on the corner and watch the patrons inside waiting impatiently for their food. Perhaps we should rest here and see if anyone drops a slice on the ground. Then we can have a quick snack and continue along with full stomachs. Mom doesn't share this sentiment and coaxes me forward, but I glance over my shoulder several times, prepared to dart back and assist in the cleanup if necessary. The restaurant doesn't have a resident dog on hand to perform that important duty, and I wonder if they're hiring.

"I live just around the corner if you need someone to monitor your floors for spills," I holler, hoping they'll take me up on the offer.

## Leslie Popp

Cars whizz by, and I wonder where everyone is going in such a hurry. There are many new faces, and I want them to know that I'm receptive to back rubs. I love cars and would gladly leap into the back seat of one of these yellow cabs and ride around the block a few times with my head out the window. There's nothing better than feeling the wind on your face and seeing the city fly by as you speed along. I like to let my tongue hang out and my ears blow back in the stiff breeze. We don't own a car, but I'm in favor of acquiring one so we could drive around the block on rainy days without getting wet, which seems incredibly useful.

We encounter one of the regular runners, a fluffy dog with a narrow face and perky ears. She's always immaculately groomed and looks ready for a fashion show. Her fur is shiny, and she's wearing a fancy pink harness that she's eager to show off. I don't know her name, and we've met so many times that it's awkward to inquire. We pause and briefly sniff each other, and I can smell the turkey kibble on her breath. She turns to Sara, and I feel myself stiffen. Mom senses my unease, and we continue down the block before I become agitated and worried. The little dog wanders away in the opposite direction, and I'm sure I'll see her again soon. I need to master my emotions and do a better job at interacting with our acquaintances. Sara isn't bothered by the encounter, and I heave a sigh of relief.

We pass a pile of trash waiting for one of those huge vehicles to rumble by with several beefy men tasked with loading the bags of decaying food and other waste into the back compartment. I tug on the leash and come to a halt beside the stinking mountain, assessing the smells and trying to decide if anything is edible and easily accessible. A variety of pungent aromas greet my nose, and I conclude that some of the food concealed within the plastic bags is fresh enough. I would like to dig through the pile and take a closer look. Who knows what treats might be lurking within this mound of discarded goods?

Mom understands exactly what I'm planning and pulls me away before I can start tearing into the flimsy bags. I'm disappointed that I couldn't investigate a single one, but as I said before, there will be another opportunity midday if they haven't collected the trash by then. Otherwise, there will be a new pile waiting for me in a few days.

We complete our circuit and approach the door of our building. The doorman hurries to open it, and I sniff his hand and offer a goofy smile to show my appreciation. He sometimes pats me on the head, which makes him alright in my book.

Leslie Popp

*Sara*

## Itty Bitty Visitor

I love making friends and am always excited to welcome fresh faces into my house. Some dogs are possessive of their homes and are skeptical or aggressive with human and animal visitors, but not me. New interactions are invigorating, and I view everyone as a potential lap to rest my head on and a face to lick. I maintain an open-door policy and invite guests to visit at any time, whether they're expected or just wish to stop by while they're in the neighborhood.

I race up to greet visitors with enthusiastic hops and vigorous wags, occasionally knocking items off the lower shelves and the coffee table. Then I leap up and try to plant slobbery kisses on their cheeks, demonstrating that one disabled leg can't hold me back from reaching my full potential. My friends have learned to anticipate this unexpected aerial feat, but new acquaintances never see it coming. Once I lick a face, you're admitted into the inner circle and are always welcome in my house.

# The Bark Diaries

My skills as a guard dog may be lacking, but that doesn't matter to me. Dad oversees home security, given he's big and strong and seems wise beyond his years. For example, he knows how to work the tricky door handles, can easily tear into a bag of kibble, and reminds me not to run into the street. He has my best interests at heart and does a fabulous job of keeping me safe and secure. I trust him completely and know that he has my back. Since he's the head of security, I can kick back, relax, and focus on being an excellent host to our beloved visitors. I roll out the welcome mat and play to my strengths.

Rachel is too timid for guard duty and enjoys appealing to guests for pets and treats. She's more hesitant and easily frightened, but as soon as I admit someone into the house, she accepts them as a trusted member of our pack.

Today, something delightful and unexpected happened. A family friend dropped by to visit and brought his itty-bitty Chihuahua to see us. I was overjoyed by this impromptu social event and plastered a welcoming grin on my face.

The man carried his tiny companion into the living room, and I raised my eyebrows in amazement. I rose to my feet and hopped across the slippery wood floor to greet our friend, sniffing his feet and legs to gather information about his whereabouts earlier today. I could tell that he had been wandering around the city and detected the faint whiff of old gum on his shoe coupled with spilled coffee on his jeans. Then I gazed up at the miniature pup in his arms and panted happily, inviting our four-legged visitor to join me on the floor for a sniff.

I was rewarded with a head massage, and I leaned against our friend's leg. He placed his companion on the floor and patted the little guy on the back. I've always thought that Chihuahuas were strange-looking dogs with oversized ears, bulgy eyes, and compact statures. Initially, I assumed they were all puppies but later learned that they were full-sized dogs. I'm still confused by this because I would expect an adult to be much larger; however, I'm determined to befriend everyone, regardless of their size and appearance. I need to be careful not to step on this little visitor or whack him with my tail because I wouldn't want our relationship to begin on a negative note.

"Hi, welcome to my house! I'm super excited to meet you. Do you want to sit on the couch? We have an extra cushion that's soft and cozy," I offered, hoping that this new acquaintance also enjoyed lounging and watching the humans. "We can lie on the floor where it's cooler if you prefer that."

The little dog tilted his head, looked me over, and began to shake. I stood there, utterly confused by this reaction and unsure how to proceed. Maybe the poor thing was cold. His fur looked thinner than mine, and while I was warm, he might be chilly. I would've been happy to cuddle together for warmth, but we'd only just met, and he didn't know me very well. I glanced over my shoulder at Rachel, who was quietly observing our visitor and looking skeptical. She's guarded and needs time to warm up to new acquaintances. I gave her a reassuring expression and panted contentedly. She took a tentative step forward before pausing again and letting me take the lead.

## The Bark Diaries

I leaned in to check on the Chihuahua's health and assess his temperature. As I drew near, the feisty little animal let out a piercing yip that startled me, causing me to jump back. The tiny dog dared to growl at me while I gazed at him in shock. He continued shivering as we all stared at each other mutely, trying to make sense of his behavior. I was only being friendly, and it was my territory, not his.

I've seen Rachel shake in response to loud noises and baths, and I concluded that the miniature dog must be terrified of me. I'm ten times his size and could easily crush him if I rolled over in my sleep. Perhaps more drastic actions were needed to show that I was harmless. I slid my front paws across the floor, lowered my belly to the ground, and sprawled out on the cool floor. I rested my head on my paws, which put me at eye level with our visitor.

The Chihuahua's ears perked up, and he hesitantly sniffed the air, shivering uncontrollably. I turned away, letting my eyes peruse the room and giving the tiny dog a moment to calm his nerves. I heard his nails click against the floor as he stepped toward me, and I tried not to make any sudden movements. He approached slowly and sniffed my paws before circling back around to my side and pausing near my rear end. I refrained from wagging my tail, knowing that it could knock him off his feet. I sighed contentedly, determined to be patient and befriend him.

Finally, the Chihuahua sat down and waited for me to make the next move. Slowly, I lifted my head and swiveled my ears toward him, signaling that I was interested in becoming better acquainted. His posture relaxed after I gently wagged my tail. I'm a very docile dog who would never harm or threaten an invited visitor. I consider myself to be the welcome party and take the job very seriously.

I was debating getting to my feet and leading the Chihuahua over to the comfy couch when his dad returned and placed a small stuffed animal at his feet. The miniature dog took one look at the furry creature and immediately leaped on it, snatching it in his jaws. He shook his head vigorously, pinned the toy between his paws, and began tearing at it relentlessly. I watched in terror as the man tossed the stuffed animal across the room, and the Chihuahua dashed after it, pouncing on its helpless form and gnawing on it before returning it to the man.

I gulped, feeling nervous and worried about the tiny beast's aggressive nature as he ripped at the toy's soft fabric and inner fluff. I hoped that he wouldn't turn his attention to me next. I wasn't sure if I had fluff on the inside, but I wasn't interested in finding out. His destructive behavior seemed unusual and unsettling.

The game continued for several minutes, and I could feel my anxiety increasing. The innocent-looking Chihuahua was proving to be a ruthless fighter, chasing a toy and punishing it for attempting to flee from his sharp teeth and powerful jaws. He yanked at its limbs and ears. Where had the shivering pup gone who had been standing in front of me only moments before? He had become a stone-cold warrior trained in the art of combat. Between the piercing yip and the deadly playtime, I was concerned about who I had welcomed into my home. Perhaps I should've screened this newcomer and stopped him at the door to conduct a background check.

## The Bark Diaries

The Chihuahua eventually tired of the game and curled up on the floor to rest. I was relieved to see him settle down but was determined to remain alert in case he targeted one of my ears or paws instead of the stuffed toy. I glanced at Rachel, whose eyes were wide with alarm, but she always looks that way. She occasionally knocks over our food bowls and is startled when they clatter against the wood floor. I reminded her that we still had a significant size advantage over the yappy pipsqueak, and I was confident that the two of us could handle him, although I would prefer not to find out.

The rest of the afternoon was spent warily eyeing the little monster that was napping in the middle of the floor. I had underestimated the pint-sized visitor and let his appearance convince me that he was a harmless puppy, instead of a mighty soldier ready to shred any unsuspecting toys.

When the Chihuahua woke from his nap, he appeared surprised to see me watching him, but what would he expect after the enthusiastic beating he gave that toy? He looked away and then back at me. Climbing to his feet, he cautiously advanced, and I worried that it was a clever trick. I grew increasingly nervous as he approached me, but I was determined not to show any fear, in case he turned out to be friendly after all. Just as he reached my tail, his dad strolled into the room, scooped him up, and made a beeline for the front door. I sighed with relief at having avoided a potential confrontation and rolled onto my side, resting my cheek against the floor. Rachel hurried to the door to ensure that the vicious pup was gone before trotting back to the couch, leaping onto her favorite cushion, and curling into a tight ball.

I was proud of how we handled the stressful situation. We maintained friendly demeanors in the face of the Chihuahua's feisty attitude. I refuse to let this incident deter me from inviting strangers into my house and will continue to roll out the welcome mat whenever someone arrives.

## Rachel

### Finders Keepers

There are many varieties of food, and I'm interested in them all, whether I like them or not. You won't know what you like unless you try new things, and some meals deserve a second chance. My golden rule is that if it makes you throw up, you should avoid it in the future, but if not, it's fair game. This method makes perfect sense and it has served me well during my years of opportunistic snacking.

I grow wiser and more worldly by the day, and over time, I've cataloged a long list of foods that are on the no list. It primarily contains random items that I've retrieved from the trash or scooped off the sidewalk, but that doesn't stop me from regularly investigating new foods. I consider myself to be an adventurous eater, and I don't understand dogs that are picky. They don't know what they're missing and are squandering opportunities to delight their taste buds. However, that's not my issue, and if they want to reject perfectly good food, then I would be happy to take it off their hands. I lick my lips just thinking about it and suddenly realize that having a picky friend could be advantageous. Imagine all the treats they might refuse to eat!

Mom is slipping on her shoes, which generally signals that it's time for a walk. I watch her closely, waiting for her to reach for the leashes. Within a few seconds, she has retrieved my woven lead and holds it out to me. I rush over, allow her to loop it around my strong neck, and pull her toward the door.

Dad joins us as we stroll out of the building and meander down the sidewalk. My parents chat cheerfully as we soak up the sun and reach the end of our normal route. To my surprise, we cross the street with purpose, which suggests that we have a special destination in mind. I love adventures and wonder where we're off to today. As long as it's not the vet, then I'm on board with their plan.

I frequently stop to sniff, analyzing the unique smells in this area. A few of the usual canine suspects make an appearance, but the scents and faces in this neighborhood are mostly unfamiliar. New experiences can be intimidating, but with Mom and Dad by my side, I know that everything will be alright.

The aroma of freshly baked bread fills my nose, and I take a long inhale. We're approaching a popular bagel joint that is supplying a steady stream of people with savory and sweet treats. I pause to sniff the door and peer in the window at the line that wraps around the counter. Everyone is playing on their phones, trying to distract themselves from their grumbling stomachs. They've certainly come to the right place to solve that problem, and I'm jealous that they're

## The Bark Diaries

minutes away from a tasty bagel. I hope that someone will share a bite with me.

Mom nudges me forward, and I begrudgingly step away from the window. Then I catch sight of something wonderful and try to contain my excitement so as not to alert the media or other dogs. A bagel smothered in cream cheese is lying beside a trash can at the end of the block. A clumsy human bought the treat, ate their fill, and then attempted to throw what was left into the trash can. Such human actions are beyond my understanding. But to my delight, they missed the bin, and the tasty morsel has no owner in sight. Today is my lucky day.

I wander along, trying to appear nonchalant and generally uninterested, but as we near the bagel, my eyes zero in on my target, and I become fixated. I can't reveal my plan, or else Mom will try to intervene. She has good intentions, but her priorities can sometimes be misguided. Clearly, someone should claim this bagel, and my nose has determined that it's still edible. Mom would say that it's unfit for consumption because it's on the ground and we don't know the previous owner. I'll devour it before she has time to react.

I watch as people pass right by the savory bite, and I pray that no one beats me to my prize. When we're a few feet away, I suddenly lunge forward, dragging Mom along behind me, and chomp down on the fragrant bread stuffed with creamy filling. The flavor is rich on my tongue, and the bread sticks to the top of my mouth, making it difficult to swallow in one gulp as I had planned. Every second it lingers in my mouth is an opportunity for Mom to pry it away from me. She moves in a circle around me to see what I've nabbed, but I turn away and chew ferociously. Finally, I manage to swallow the last crumb, feeling satisfied with myself and proud that I accomplished the heist.

Dad kneels and peers into my mouth, and I'm happy to oblige now that it's empty. He glances at Mom and shakes his head, and she shrugs in response, understanding that I've won this round. We continue walking, and my eyes sweep the sidewalk for any unclaimed food that is seeking an owner. It's a finders-keepers situation in my opinion. Mom and Dad are on alert and have grown wise to my strategy. I can only execute a stunt like that once on each walk before they begin to watch me intently and scan the sidewalk ahead for any stray food. I'm temporarily satisfied with my treat, so it doesn't bother me. I'll have another opportunity on the midnight stroll anyway.

We pause in front of another food establishment, and I sniff the air enthusiastically, trying to determine if the cuisine is of interest. Spicy scents greet my nose, and I wonder if the strong flavors would upset my stomach. I'll try anything once. Dad takes my leash, and Mom disappears into the restaurant. I would like to accompany her, but I've learned over the years that dogs aren't allowed in these businesses. The rule is completely absurd, but I've come to accept it. I press my face to the glass door, tracking Mom's every move to ensure that she's safe.

Dad pulls me back when another patron approaches, and I follow him to the edge of the sidewalk and out of the flow of foot traffic. We wait patiently, and I wonder what Mom is doing. I wish that she would finish soon because I don't like being separated from her. I'm becoming more anxious with every passing minute. Doors pose a real challenge for me, and I haven't figured out how to work the handles with my fluffy paws. I think about it daily but have yet to devise a successful strategy for addressing the issue. The handles are inconveniently located and are installed too high for me to grab with my teeth. It would be much more convenient if every door was equipped with a doggy entrance. I don't know why this isn't the standard already.

I watch unfamiliar people wander by, wondering where they're going in such a hurry. Don't they know that Mom is in that building, and we can't go anywhere until she returns? They could wait with me while scratching behind my ears, and I would appreciate that gesture. My schedule is flexible, and I'm open to making friends. You never know where you'll meet kind people who are willing to rub your back and massage your ears, so it's important to enhance your cuteness in public and encourage others to approach you. While I'm always nervous, I make sure to open my eyes wide, tilt my ears forward, and let my mouth hang open to mimic a smile.

I want everyone to know that I'm a friendly dog just looking to meet new people on this glorious afternoon. I enjoy long walks, kibble or any other available food, and afternoon naps beside my favorite humans. All outstretched hands and unsuspecting butts are subject to sniffing. How can I get to know my neighbors without investigating their scents? Humans never attempt to sniff my butt, which seems odd to me; however, I'm not about to change my tactics at this age, and it's still trending in the canine community.

Perhaps humans will catch on one day, given I regularly demonstrate this greeting ritual.

The door of the building opens, and Mom emerges carrying a brown bag with two flimsy handles. I prance around, glad that she's safe and has rejoined our pack. While I love family outings in the city, I prefer to stay together as a unit. That's not always possible, given dogs are not allowed inside certain buildings. Mom lovingly pats my head, and I eagerly plunge my nose into the bag to assess her acquisition. She pulls it away, but not before I catch the delicious aroma of brown rice, roasted vegetables, and tofu, coupled with a pungent array of spices that tickle the inside of my nose. It's Thai food!

I have limited experience with this cuisine because the spices don't agree with my digestive system, and onion and garlic are toxic to dogs. Nevertheless, it carries a distinct scent that lingers in the apartment for hours, and I salivate more than usual. I appreciate Mom and Dad being cautious and ensuring that I only consume food that won't harm me; I might be willing to take a risk with the onions. In fact, I would gladly eat the entire bounty if they opened the containers and set them on the ground.

We return to our apartment after another successful hunt for sustenance. Mom can always find the best food and periodically brings me along on retrieval missions. I'm always excited to accompany her on these outings because I want my family to be well-fed and healthy. I need Mom and Dad to live forever so they can open bags of kibble, given my paws are not up for the task. I've yet to master the complicated sealing system used on the bags. If we ever run out of food, I can simply stroll down the street to this gourmet kitchen and request a meal. Dad would never let the kibble train run dry, though, so this scenario seems unlikely. I want to be prepared and have a backup plan ready, just in case.

    I lead Mom and Dad home, memorizing the route to this restaurant, stopping to sniff every trash can, and hoping for another stray bagel bite. Alas, I find nothing, and it seems that other dogs or humans have beaten me to these coveted snacks.

Leslie Popp

*Rachel*

**Where There is Rain, There Are Puddles**

Rain is pouring from an angry-looking sky, making me feel lethargic. I lie on the living room floor and gaze out the window as the wind thrashes the trees and blows the leaves into a swirling tornado. Drops of water batter the glass and roll down like nature's tears. I sigh heavily and wonder why Mother Nature periodically revolts against us, forcing us to take shelter in our cozy homes and press our noses to the window. I try to predict when the sun will shine again.

On days like this, I focus on napping, stretching, and snuggling with Mom and Dad. I'm grateful to have this comfortable couch and can't imagine the hardships faced by those street dogs. It's depressing to think about. Mom and Dad often venture out in the rain, and I feel sorry for them because they always return looking cold and damp. No one should have to brave this weather, and instead, we should spend the day together. I wag my tail thinking about the belly rubs that I would receive if my parents stayed by my side and waited for the sun to emerge. I would hope for rain every day.

# The Bark Diaries

I try to meditate, letting the sound of the rain lull me into a calm stupor, but then I think about those pesky drops splattering onto my fur and tremble. I'm a Labrador Retriever mix, and yes, we're supposed to be water dogs who love swimming and being wet, but I didn't inherit that gene. I'm terrified of taking baths and dislike the rain. When I think about plunging into the river nearby, it makes me shiver and shake with fear. I'm a land-loving dog that is content to leave the water-related tasks to someone better suited for that job. Sara shares my views, which makes me feel less self-conscious. She has thick fur that takes all day to dry, too.

Unfortunately, sleep remains elusive, so I rise to my feet and assume a downward dog pose, stretching my front paws out, leaning back, and keeping my rear end raised. My face scrunches up in an adorable expression, causing Mom to stop what she's doing, scramble for her phone, and quickly snap a photo. Stretching is good for my back and keeps me limber. I'm not very flexible, but I've mastered this yoga pose, and Mom sometimes mimics the position. She often rolls out a colorful mat and assumes a sequence of poses while listening to soothing music. I like to sit nearby and observe her technique, wagging my tail when she executes the downward dog stretch.

"That's my move!" I pant excitedly. "You're doing a great job today. Just breathe slowly and lean back a bit more."

I scoot closer so she can rub my neck, and we focus on our breathing and try to improve the stretch. These are beautiful moments between the two of us. Sara frequently barges in during Mom's workouts and attempts to lick her face and stand on the mat, forcing Mom to hunker down and defend her space. If she's unsuccessful, then we have to conclude yoga for the day. Once Sara flops down, you have to drag her off, and she'll chase the mat around the room if you attempt to reposition it. She's a stubborn dog who knows exactly what she wants.

Sitting on the floor is an invitation for face licks, and there's no way around it. Sara will hop or crawl into striking range, and Mom will watch her warily, attempting to dodge Sara's tongue when she lunges forward for a wet kiss. I enjoy observing the game and placing bets on who will win. Sara is crafty, but Mom is on high alert and never takes her eyes off that lolling tongue. She must react swiftly to avoid the slobber. For entertainment, I sit nearby and keep score, content to let Mom exercise and pet me on her own time, instead of barging in and demanding attention.

After yoga, we lie on the couch and stare at the TV, which depicts a sunny day and a group of laughing friends. They look like trustworthy people, and their yard is lovely. It's full of vibrant flowers, and there's even a squirrel in the background. Their couch is inviting, and they have a fluffy rug in the living room that seems ideal for naps. I would love to have a humongous rug that covers the entire room. Just to be clear, I enjoy the floor, but nothing beats a plush rug. I'll have to ask Mom for one as a birthday present, although if I'm forced to choose, I would prefer extra treats. If she could open the bag of chewy morsels, place it at my feet, and walk away, that would be ideal. I'm not sure if my puppy heart

## The Bark Diaries

could process the sheer joy that would accompany this kind gesture.

I shake my head, attempting to dispel thoughts of open treat bags. I don't know when my birthday is, but it's not today, and I don't want to fixate on treats for lunch when that's unlikely. I should probably cut back on my snacks, given I'm a bit stocky, but I love kibble, and the extra insulation serves me well in the bitter New York winters. I could slim down for summer by giving up my tasty food, but that would be a shame. I'm content with having extra padding around my middle. No one has criticized my body type, and I'm not self-conscious. Sara's build is leaner, and she needs to stay light and fit to help with her ungainly step, so I'm more than willing to eat any extra food.

Mom strides over to the small basket where we store the leashes, and I leap to my feet in anticipation. I trot over to investigate and circle her as she tries to loop one around my neck. Sara quickly joins in, and we give Mom the run around. The idea of a family walk makes me giddy. Mom prepares for the walk by jamming her feet into the sneakers by the door, and we're off on our next adventure.

When we reach the lobby, I come to an abrupt halt and gaze forlornly at the gray day. Distracted by the thought of a peaceful walk, I temporarily forgot that it was pouring rain outside. I failed to consider that it would involve getting wet. Sara looks uncertain, standing at the threshold of the building and assessing the drenched sidewalk. The street is quiet, and the world seems to move slower on rainy days. I do appreciate the privacy it allows us on outings.

## Leslie Popp

Mom opens the black umbrella that shields her from the rain and steps bravely onto the sidewalk. I cautiously follow her lead, and Sara lopes along beside me. The downpour has slowed to a depressing drizzle, and I hope it doesn't soak through my outer layer of fur. We progress slowly down the block, pausing so Sara can investigate one of the waterlogged flower boxes. No birds are chirping today, and the wind chills my nose, which is peppered with small droplets. I squint my eyes, hating the feel of the light spray coating me from tail to paw.

Dutifully, I continue the march, only once becoming distracted by an intriguing whiff from a light pole. Another dog was here recently, and I pause to decode the message it left behind. I suppose we can spare thirty seconds. Then we encounter a muddy puddle that has formed along the curb, and my heart leaps in excitement. I hurry over and drink greedily from the murky water, gulping down mouthfuls of fresh rain mixed with street dirt. Mom quickly pulls me back, but I tug on my leash, wanting a few more sips. Doesn't she know that puddles are the best water sources, with minerals from the road and complex flavors that are exotic and intriguing? They're nature's water bowls that are created for our enjoyment, and I'm happy to share them with others.

I've never seen Mom or Dad drink from puddles, but that's their loss. They don't know what they're missing, and I'll happily lap up their share. Between the extra food from Sara and the additional water from my parents, I'll be one well-fed and hydrated pup.

Mom leads me away from the puddle, and I relinquish control before spotting another appealing puddle ahead and formulating a plan to plunge my nose into it before she has time to react. There are an abundance of puddle-drinking opportunities on our walk, and I try to take advantage of them, but Mom is aware of my intentions and manages to steer me away. Puddles linger for a few hours, and now that I've mapped them out, I'll have a more creative plan of attack for tonight's walk.

I arrive back at the front door of our building, and suddenly realize how wet I am after being solely focused on my puddle-related mission. Now that we're in the lobby, I feel the dampness seeping in, and I shake vigorously, sending water flying in all directions. Sara does the same, causing her fur to stick up at odd angles. Mom should brush us so we're styled in the latest fashion. No one likes a messy fur day, and I lack the dexterity to brush myself.

Returning to the apartment, I lie down to rest after the excursion and cook up a new strategy for those tempting puddles. My mouth falls open in a half smile as I think about the evening walk and the gritty street water waiting for me.

Leslie Popp

*Sara*

## I Decline Rainy Days

My hearing is exceptional. When I'm casually lounging on the cool tile floor, I'm actually carefully analyzing sounds that are echoing through the apartment. I track the cars rumbling down the street, the neighbors chatting, the ding of the elevator in the hallway, and the sound of Dad breathing. Having him close by gives me a sense of peace and tranquility.

I've been eavesdropping on the women next door, who always say hi to me when we cross paths in the hallway. They're about Mom's age and greet me with big smiles and bubbly personalities. They often return home late at night, and I'm familiar with the sound of their voices and their light footsteps down the carpeted hallway. I'm focused on my social standing in the building, and I go out of my way to say hello to everyone and offer a welcoming gaze.

Dad's hearing is inferior to mine, and it's easy to sneak up on him when he's focused on the TV or his phone. This tactic would never succeed with me because I can hear someone approaching from the moment they step off the elevator. My floppy ears are soft and adorable, but they are also incredible tools for monitoring the neighborhood for suspicious activity.

I keep up with local events by monitoring the sounds that drift through the windows. I can recognize individual dogs by their barks and the unique tones of the voices of their humans. I know when the truck filled with letters and packages arrives and begins unloading its bounty. I always hope that it's delivering more dog food, although that only happens once a month. I know how hard the wind is blowing by the leaves rustling on the tree outside, and I certainly know when it's raining by the ping of the small drops against the glass panes. Perhaps I should become a meteorologist and announce the changes in weather throughout the day. It seems simple enough to confirm, "We are experiencing heavy winds, but the sun is still shining."

Today, I'm lounging on the couch and listening to the pitter-patter of raindrops. I strongly dislike the rain even though I'm allegedly classified as a water dog. I prefer to remain dry and warm in my cozy apartment and ignore rainy days, opting to snooze away the afternoon. I sigh, remembering the uncomfortable feel of waterlogged fur against my skin. No, thank you!

I hear Dad roll out of bed and listen to his footsteps as he gets dressed. A few minutes later, he emerges into the living room, and I excitedly lift my head, wag my tail, and beam a smile at him. He slept for hours, and I'm overjoyed to see him. He's not a morning person and is struggling to awaken from his restful slumber. Dad retrieves the colorful leashes from a basket on the shelf.

Rachel springs to her feet and bounces from one side of the couch to the other, pausing beside me. She pants enthusiastically and wags her tail in anticipation. We both love walks, but I usually decline strolls in the rain. I don't want to venture outside on days when the sky is rebelling against us and pouring water on the world below. I'll wait for the next walk and hope that the weather is more cooperative by then. If not, then I'll be forced to go outside because I would never use the bathroom in my own home. That's not what a good dog would do, and I want to be a good dog.

Rachel bounds to the floor and prances over to Dad, circling him and exuding pure delight at the prospect of a walk. She doesn't pay attention to the weather and is always willing to go outside. Rachel spins around and around, and Dad struggles to loop the leash over her head. She's obviously excited, and I absolutely understand the sentiment on sunny days. I'm comfortable on my cushion and will remain entrenched in this spot until the sound of the pinging drops fades away.

Rachel finally allows the leash to slip over her head, and a triumphant look crosses Dad's face. He advances toward me, holding the other leash and calling my name. He pats his leg, which is a sign that he wants me to hop up, but I hold my ground and rest my head on my paws. I raise my eyebrows and wait for his next move. He gently rubs my back, causing my tail to wag vigorously, and holds the leash in front of my face, but I keep my chin firmly planted on my paws. He tries to slide the leash over my head, but I won't allow it. The rain makes the morning walk a solid no for me. I can hold it until the midday outing.

Dad says my name again, and I gaze up at his imploring face. Rachel paces and tilts her head at me in question. Clearly, she hasn't assessed the weather. Dad then physically lifts my head, slips the leash around my neck, and lightly tugs on the rope, but I still refuse to concede my position. How do I make him understand that the day is dreary, and I have no desire to abandon this cozy spot? The couch is soft, and I would prefer to remain curled up on my favorite cushion while the two of them scout the neighborhood and report back on any captivating findings.

Finally, Dad lets out an exasperated sigh and moves to my side with a look of determination. He kneels on the couch and slides both hands underneath me. Realizing that he's about to lift me onto my feet, I leap up and slide awkwardly to the floor, giving Dad a confused look. I dislike being carried, and I could tell where that was going. He must desperately need me to accompany him, so I begrudgingly trudge toward the door.

Rachel is excited and sniffs at my face while we wait for the elevator. When we reach the lobby, my heart sinks as I stare out at the dreary day, and Rachel pauses at the front door as reality sets in. She ignored my weather report and now appears disheartened. My heart goes out to her because she's always so enthusiastic about walks but is surprisingly unaware when it comes to storms.

I gaze up at the gray sky and watch the pesky droplets stream down the windows, forming puddles on the sidewalk. Dad throws open the door and pulls the hood of his jacket over his head. I wish that I had one of those to protect my fur from the unwelcome liquid. Perhaps I can borrow Mom's next time. I bet it would fit me if I slipped my front legs through the armholes and left it hanging open around my stomach. I would be the most stylish pup in Manhattan. I've seen other dogs trotting around the neighborhood in coats and sweaters, so my new fashion would fit right in.

"Okay, are we doing this?" I ask Rachel. "We could go back to the apartment and try again this evening. I don't have to go right now. I mean, I do, but I'll hold it."

Rachel looks miserable, but is signaling that she needs to use the bathroom while backpedaling about going outside in the rain. She despises water more than I do, but a dog must do what a dog must do. There's no way we're peeing in the house because that is strictly forbidden, and I wouldn't want to disappoint Mom or Dad over a self-induced accident. I take a deep breath and step through the door, feeling a spray of water against my face.

"Let's do it!" I call, boldly venturing out and discovering that the drizzle is more of an annoyance than a true impediment.

Rachel follows my lead and plods along with her head down. While she initially looks distressed, she's quickly distracted by her desire to sniff every light pole. She likes to be thorough on walks and ensure that we gather information about our canine neighbors. She guides us toward a murky puddle and begins to greedily lap up the water before Dad pulls her away. We have clean water at home, but the sidewalk water is a delicious brand that's worth sampling from time to time.

# The Bark Diaries

I'm very particular about where I relieve myself, and I prefer the middle of a crosswalk, holding up traffic and showing those honking cars who's boss. Dad doesn't approve of this habit and looks nervous every time we cross a street. I choose a different location on each walk and search for a spot that feels right. The rain makes this task more difficult because I try not to wander too far from our building, but I also don't want to pee in my front yard.

We patrol the block, stopping to sniff, scouting for street food, and sneaking drinks from puddles. Finally, I see the perfect spot and pause in the middle of a crosswalk to squat before a line of cars that are waiting patiently for the light to change. It's convenient because they can also wait for me to do my business. They're in my territory now.

Dad holds his hand up and looks sheepishly at the drivers who wave back. He fumbles with a small bag, scoops my droppings off the asphalt, and ushers us to the other side of the street. The cars rush forward as soon as my paws touch the sidewalk.

Dad lobs the bag into the garbage can on the corner, sinking a perfect shot. He lifts both hands in victory, and a sense of pride wells up in my chest. He's incredible! His aim is the best on our side of town and possibly in the entire city. We practice this every day, using the neighborhood trash cans as goals and our fragrant baggies as the balls. Dad has perfected his underhand swing and can catapult the weighted sacks through the air and into the cans without ever touching the rims. It's a valuable skill, and I'm proud of his physical abilities in this department.

## Leslie Popp

A car races through a nearby puddle, and water splatters the sidewalk, causing Rachel and me to scamper out of the way. I hobble as quickly as I can on my disabled leg, which is not fast enough. My tail is peppered with the spray, and I shake vigorously, sending water droplets flying in every direction. Dad holds up his hands in a futile attempt to shield himself. We're already wet, so he shouldn't mind the additional soaking.

I lick my nose, savoring the cool drops running down my snout. Rachel turns toward home and leads the way. Her butt sways at head height, and her tail nearly whacks me in the face. I pick up my pace and trot alongside her, stopping to sniff a bike rack and each street lamp along the way. We move methodically, tangling our leashes and occasionally wrapping them around Dad's legs. I don't possess good spatial awareness because I'm distracted by the alluring smells, which complicates family walks. It doesn't bother me if it slows us down because I've got time on my paws.

We return to our building, and I give another energetic shake in the elevator, which causes Dad to turn away. My fur is sticking up at odd angles, but that's okay. I'm still adorable and will soon be dry and fluffy again.

Once inside the apartment, I gulp down the fresh water in my bowl, which lacks the unique undertones of street water, and flop down on the floor, leaving wet paw prints behind. I hope the downpour concludes before the afternoon walk because I dislike the damp feel of my fur and would prefer not to repeat our experience in the rain. However, if Rachel needs another stroll, I'll go with her, as we're inseparable, and I feel lonely without her. I'll brave any storm to be with her.

Leslie Popp

## Rachel

### The Park Downstairs

If you haven't been to a park, then you should prioritize finding the nearest one and sniffing the perimeter. There's something wonderful about an open area where dogs and people can bask in the afternoon sunshine. In my opinion, we should build parks on every block for the convenience of all dogs and humans. Who wouldn't want to live beside a green space with trees, flowers, and dogs galore?

Today is one of the two glorious days of the week when Mom and Dad can sleep in and forego those annoying alarms. The noise startles me every morning and heightens my anxiety because it sounds like an ominous warning that something has gone terribly wrong, and we need to wake up and flee. I've become accustomed to it over time but am never able to sleep through the racket. However, the alarm means that Mom is about to roll out of bed, which is always welcome news. I'm eager to see her each morning as she emerges from the bedroom. I wait patiently on the couch until she extends her hand to me. That's my cue to rush over

## The Bark Diaries

for some pets and to show how much I love and appreciate her.

Days without a blaring alarm bring the prospect of an exciting afternoon at the park. Dad attaches my leash for our midday stroll, and I make a beeline toward my favorite green space as we exit the building. Dad obliges and guides me safely across the street because I forgot to look both ways again. I need to work on that, but it's never a priority when there are alluring smells, crumbs of discarded food on the ground, strange people and dogs about, and a special outing to focus on.

We trot along until we reach the metal gates that mark the park's entrance. I wag my tail enthusiastically as Dad swings open the gate and then promptly drag him inside, nearly tripping over Sara in the process. She hovers her nose an inch from the ground and begins to sniff purposefully, wandering about and winding her leash around Dad's legs. He's forced to quickly extricate himself before Sara pulls the lead tight and binds his knees together. She lacks awareness of her surroundings and often hopelessly tangles our leashes. When the birds are chirping and the air is full of intriguing sounds and smells, she becomes distracted and expects the rest of us to follow wherever she leads. This questionable habit is not usually an issue, given our interests are aligned, and I'm happy to let her forge a path while I sniff the area.

I survey the park, watching the leaves on a nearby bush blow gently in the breeze while tugging Dad along to investigate. There are a host of smells from the neighborhood dogs strolling this route and their owners sitting on the nearby benches. I plunge my head into a bush, searching for anything of interest, but there are only more leaves and some prickly branches, so I move along. The flowers are blooming, and I pee on one to mark it as my own. It's a lovely color, appears healthy and strong, and stretches up toward the sun at about my chin height. I take a long sniff, and the scent tickles the inside of my nose. I take a step back as I let out a powerful sneeze and shake my head in embarrassment at being startled by my bodily functions.

Movement near the next tree interrupts my thoughts, and I lock my eyes on the group of strutting pigeons parading through the garden. They look so confident, like they're trying to claim this section of the park for themselves. They travel in an intimidating gang, and I'm tempted to concede this space. However, barking at pigeons is one of life's amazing joys. Generally, I'm a quiet and subdued pup, but when pigeons are involved, I can't help myself.

Sara spots our feathered friends, and we launch a coordinated attack, dragging Dad behind us as we advance toward our targets. The pigeons are surprisingly brave and initially hold their position as we draw near, perhaps preparing to square off and overwhelm us with their numbers. I've seen them posture before and they won't fool me this time. I'm determined to capture one of these crafty foes and keep it as a pet. We can tie it to my collar and let it hop beside me or perch on my back, given it also favors the outdoors.

When we're a few feet away, the mob of birds erupts into flight. I bark excitedly and strain against my leash, wanting to dart after them and feeling certain that if I had a bit more runway, then I could easily nab one right out of the air. I've tried to capture a pigeon on numerous occasions and have failed, but I love the thrill of the chase. Each time it seems as though I'm only a hair shy of claiming my prize. I pace, waiting for one to plummet into my clutches, but they fly away to the far end of the park. I'm out of breath and pause to glance at Sara and regroup.

She has accepted defeat and is busy inspecting the area where the birds were lounging. I follow suit, and my nose twitches at their unique scent.

"Until next time, my feathered opponents," I call over my shoulder. "Don't get too comfortable."

Feeling triumphant, I turn my attention to the benches and flower beds. A gleaming acorn catches my eye, and I scarf it down before Dad can intervene. I've developed a taste for acorns, which are a rare delicacy in my book. Those pesky squirrels may hoard most of them, but when I manage to get my paws on one, I gulp it down in an instant. The nutty, earthy flavor awakens something primal in me, as if I'm a wild dog foraging and conquering the great outdoors. Sure, there's kibble waiting at home, but it never brings the same sense of satisfaction. Besides, I've proven my survival skills with three acorns foraged on this outing alone.

The other thing you should know about the park is that it's always packed with dogs. I'm a calm and loving dog toward people, but unfamiliar canines make me anxious, and I'm on alert when meeting other neighborhood residents. There's a designated fenced area where we can run off-leash and play with our four-legged friends. Dad leads us toward that space, and we slip through the double gate, carefully closing it behind us.

Now, it's time to socialize, and a wave of anxiety washes over me. Dad removes my leash, and I feel awkward without the tether. We always use leashes when we're outdoors, and it's an unfamiliar sensation. It's not my first time in the dog run, but I have to acclimate to the new faces and the freedom to stray from Dad's side. I remain close to him in case trouble arises, whether I need to protect him, or he needs to protect me.

I take a deep breath and follow Sara as she explores the area. She's more relaxed, though she still watches the other dogs closely. We stroll along the fence, examining the perimeter and assessing the crowd. The park is full of familiar faces and a few new ones too. I watch as a woman tosses a tennis ball high into the air, and an athletic-looking pup races after it, catching it after a single bounce. The black dog chews the ball for a moment before the woman whistles, instantly capturing his attention. He glances up and races back to her, dropping the ball neatly at her feet. They repeat the routine several times, and it reminds me of the game that Mom plays in our apartment. Perhaps I should start throwing the ball for her so she doesn't have to play alone. The pup is focused on his task, and I can't help but wonder why he brings the ball back to his human only to have it tossed away again. If he simply kept it, he wouldn't need to chase it down each time. It's an odd game, and instead of joining in, I prefer to watch from a safe distance.

Then an elegant Husky snatches the tennis ball and darts away. The black pup gives chase, clearly upset at losing his toy. The Husky's powerful legs carry him just out of reach as he tears around the park, the black pup barking angrily at

## The Bark Diaries

his heels. They weave in between startled people and dogs until the Husky skids to a stop and whirls around to face his pursuer. A low growl rumbles from his chest as he stands tall, tail high, ears angled forward, and the fur along his spine bristling. The ball remains firmly in his jaws, and he gives the younger dog a warning look. The pup paces, steps forward, then retreats—determined to reclaim the ball but wary of challenging his formidable opponent.

Suddenly, a man jogs up to the Husky, holds his collar, and orders him to drop the ball. The Husky tilts his head, hesitant to surrender his prize. The black pup barks enthusiastically, and the man repeats the command. Slowly, the Husky lowers his head and lets the ball tumble from his jaws. He appears forlorn as his owner leads him away, allowing the pup to reclaim the ball, retreat to his owner, and recover from the daunting encounter. This, I decide, is why I don't play ball.

The black pup suddenly sprints toward me, catching me off guard and forcing me to retreat. It sniffs me from head to tail, and I freeze. The abrupt approach unsettles me; and while the pup doesn't seem aggressive, I prefer a more polite introduction. It circles eagerly, leaning too close to my face for comfort. I leap back and let out a low growl, which immediately puts Sara on alert. She echoes my growl, standing beside me to show that we mean business. The pup blinks, tilts its head, and then trots away to find someone else to play with.

I relax and exhale a shaky breath. I didn't mean to be rude or frighten my four-legged neighbor, but his close proximity made me uneasy. The pup's boundless energy was overwhelming. I've always preferred older dogs who amble over calmly, connect with your eyes, and make their intentions clear before leaning in for a friendly sniff.

I retreat to Dad's side and sit by his feet, content to observe the activity from a safe distance. Sara wanders around with her nose to the ground, unconcerned with the noisy barking and animals racing about. The black pup scurries next to her, ready to attempt another introduction, and Sara watches him hop around before continuing on her way. He takes this action as an invitation to remain by her side and begins to sniff as well. He accidentally startles Sara, and she barks animatedly, causing me to leap to my feet and hurry over to defend my sister. Dad follows and pats us reassuringly. The pup steps back, but Dad strides forward and extends his hand. The little guy scampers over, and Dad scratches him behind the ears, receiving a slobbery lick in return.

Dad senses that the activity is too much for my delicate nerves, so he leads us out of the dog run. The moment he attaches my leash and takes charge again, I feel reassured and happily follow his lead. We pass through the double gates and meander toward the far end of the park.

Several flights of stairs lead up to the street, and although Sara's limp prevents us from going down them, she can manage the climb up. I'll admit, stairs aren't my cup of tea either, but they provide good strength training.

I pause to assess the steep slope, gauging the height of each step. Taking a deep breath, I race up as fast as I can, dragging Dad behind me. He grips my leash in one hand and Sara's in the other as she approaches the stairs at a steadier pace. I glance back, watching her closely, fearing she'll lose her balance. Step by step, she reaches the top, panting heavily from the effort, but clearly proud of herself. Pride swells in me too, and I wag my tail, letting my sister know she has done an excellent job. I'm genuinely impressed by her determination. We all deserve a few treats to celebrate her achievement.

I point my nose toward home, savoring the satisfaction of another successful park day. I chased the pigeons with all my energy, inspected every tree with care, handled the encounter with the energetic pup, and mastered the stairs. Still, I know I have to work on my social interactions with inquisitive dogs. My first instinct is to be defensive, but I suspect they're only trying to play. None of us are perfect, after all, and I'll keep practicing my greetings. I want to be known as a good dog, and good dogs don't growl at curious puppies.

Leslie Popp

*Rachel*

## We Love to Pawty

I love pawties! I feel happiest when friends fill the house with smiles, shower me with attention, and pile on the compliments. I relish spending quality time with them and appreciate every visit.

I know that tonight is a pawty night because Mom is diligently arranging trays of snacks, and Dad is frantically cleaning up. I don't know why we're concerned with hiding dirty clothes and folding the blankets on the couch. Those clothes give the place character, and I enjoy the faint smell of sweat. The blankets are soft and cozy, and we're just going to unfold them once everyone leaves, so tidying up seems like a waste of time.

I sit patiently by the table and monitor the food preparation, hoping that a tasty morsel will fall to the floor. Mom is careful not to spill anything, but I'm sure there will be accidents later; I can already sense the clean-up chaos brewing.

Dad drags the vacuum out of the closet, and I watch it with suspicion. It's loud, forceful, and downright intimidating. That awful machine should live outside where it can't bother us again. Dad plugs it in, and the vacuum roars to life, tugging him around the room as it scours every inch of the floor.

Sara and I retreat to the bedroom to escape the disturbing noise, and I cower in the corner, hoping that it will be over soon. She lies by my side, looking similarly distraught and unsure what to do. We could dismantle the screeching machine before its next use, and maybe Dad will be unable to find a replacement, but it resides in the hall closet and is not easily accessible.

The terrifying device appears in the doorway, and I leap to my feet, glancing around for a place to hide, but it's blocking the only exit. Suddenly, it goes quiet, and Dad rolls it into the bedroom and attaches the cord to another panel on the wall. Sara and I race back to the living room and seek refuge on the couch, which is beyond the vacuum's reach. I've never seen it climb on furniture and have concluded that it's incapable of leaving the ground, which is a relief.

The device roars to life, and I drop my head onto my paws, trying to ignore the sound. It traverses the bedroom, rummaging through our things and clearing them out of the way. It's an intrusive process with the unsavory machine peering under the bed, rearranging the shoes on the floor, and threatening the edge of any blanket brave enough to dangle off the bed. The noise is abrasive to my ears and gets under my fur. I bury my head in my paws and try to think comforting thoughts about treats, lost bagel bites, snuggle time with Mom, and evening walks with Dad on warm days. They temporarily distract me, but the vacuum's bellows shatter the tranquil images. I attempt to refocus and glance at Sara for reassurance. She lowers her head and raises her eyebrows in concern. She wraps her tail around herself protectively and is pretending that the vacuum is a figment of her imagination.

Then the apartment is quiet again, and I sigh, lifting my head to watch Dad roll the offensive machine back into the closet and lock it away where it can't disturb us. He kneels beside Sara and me and lovingly rubs our backs, sensing that we were unsettled. I don't want to appear anxious and scared when the pawty guests arrive. I'm usually bubbly and ready to lick everyone's hands and accept endless pets and compliments.

The food is out, the place is sparkling, Mom and Dad are nicely dressed, and I'm prepared to greet my friends. I leap up at the first knock and trot over to stand beside Mom as she opens the door. Her face lights up, and she embraces our visitor. I lean forward to sniff the woman's pants and shoes, finding that her scent is familiar. The newcomer rubs my head and plants a kiss on my brow before Sara muscles in and demands attention. I reposition myself by the door to wait for the next guest because a gracious host greets everyone personally and ensures that they feel welcome. I take good manners very seriously and want to ensure that this gathering is a success.

A steady stream of old and new friends crosses our threshold, and I catalog their smells and lick all outstretched hands. I hold my floppy ears forward and wag my tail to show how thrilled I am and how much I want to be friends. If they're Mom and Dad's friends, then they're mine as well!

## The Bark Diaries

When the rush subsides, I leave my post at the door and mingle with our visitors, covertly sniffing a few butts as I meander through the crowd. I nuzzle several hands and hope that someone will offer me a snack. I find myself surrounded by a group of adoring women who want to pose for photos with me. This is one of my favorite activities, so I sit calmly and hold my head high as they crouch beside me in turn. I take the opportunity to press my nose into their palms and against their cheeks, eliciting giggles and hugs in return. I've mastered the Instagram photo shoot and use it to my advantage. The women fawn over me, and once they're satisfied with the pictures, I roll onto my back and request a belly rub. One woman coos, kneels, and begins to massage my tummy. I lie perfectly still, all four feet in the air, letting her rub my soft fur. It's pure bliss; I could stay like this forever. When she pauses, I wiggle around, flailing my legs until someone else steps in to take her place.

Then it's time to assess the food spread, which is drawing significant attention. I wander beneath the table to check for any snacks that are on the loose without an owner and discover that a chip has escaped from its bowl. I swallow it quickly before someone else claims it and then continue scanning the area. My nose leads me toward the kitchen, and I lap up a bit of cheese that must have leaped from someone's plate. I slurp up a sugary puddle from a careless cup and start thinking about dessert. I hope it's peanut butter cookies; my absolute favorite.

I gaze at the crowd, my tail wagging eagerly. So many dog lovers have gathered, and I can hardly believe that they all came to see me. I'm a well-behaved dog and fortunate to have such an enthusiastic fan club.

I hear a loud thump and whirl around to discover that someone has bumped into the food table, sending pretzels cascading down to the floor. I race over and begin hoovering them up, to the delight of everyone in the vicinity. They stare at me and smile, which confirms that I'm doing an excellent job of keeping the apartment in impeccable order. I want to make a great impression and show our guests a tidy house, so we must quickly clean up any spills. I suspect they're admiring my speed and work ethic, and I take a moment to bask in their praise. A kind man rubs my neck, saying, "What a good girl!" while another woman exclaims, "You're such a sweetheart!" My mouth stretches into a grin, and I pant softly, thinking about all the wonderful friends I have.

I search the crowd for Mom and spot her disappearing into the bathroom, so I stroll over and assume a sentry position by the door. Despite having a house full of dog-friendly individuals, I want to remind her that she's still my favorite person. I wouldn't want her to feel slighted because I'm spending time with other people and licking their hands like I've known them for years. Mom is my priority, and I always check in with her throughout the night.

She emerges a few minutes later, and I leap with excitement. She kneels beside me and offers a gentle hug, which makes me want to crawl onto her lap. I'm too big for that, but I still dream about it. I wag my tail enthusiastically and breathe in the flowery scent of her long hair. She pulls away, scratches behind my ears, and we proceed back into the fray to mingle with our guests.

# The Bark Diaries

I attach myself to a woman who is chattering excitedly and feeding me pieces of shortbread cookies from her plate. They're not as good as the peanut butter kind, but they're still delicious, and I'll happily sit here with my mouth open while she loads more in. When she gets up for a refill, I look pleadingly at the rest of the group, but no one offers me another cookie. No matter, I've already had at least three, and with the pretzels, cheese, and chips from earlier, I'm satisfied with the night's haul. My taste buds are delighted by the many delicacies, and maybe there will be leftovers to share tomorrow.

Sara sidles up beside me, and I smell something salty on her breath. Clearly, she hopped on the treat train as well, and I'm glad that our visitors have been so generous. She limps off to slobber on several enthusiastic partygoers.

The evening is filled with laughter, indulgent treats, abundant back rubs, and a cheerful atmosphere, but after hours of socializing, I'm entirely worn out. My paws are weary, and my eyes are beginning to droop because my bedtime was hours ago. I make one last round to say goodnight to our friends, then retreat to the bedroom and curl up on the cool floor where I can relax in relative peace and quiet. Mom wanders in and plants a tender kiss on the top of my head, wishing me sweet dreams. I gaze up at her groggily, give a sleepy wag, and drift off into a much-needed slumber.

Leslie Popp

*Sara*

## Please Hand Me My Food

I enjoy a wide variety of foods, including dry kibble, crunchy and soft treats, wet canned meals, table scraps, and the occasional abandoned morsel on the sidewalk, which I consider a delicacy. However, my favorite food is anything offered from Dad's hand. The flavor matters less than how it's delivered, because when I lap the tasty meal from his palm and lick the remnants from his fingers, we share a quiet, special moment. His attention belongs entirely to me, and that's why I insist on being served this way.

Today, I'm lounging on the couch watching the pictures flicker across the noisy TV. The voices emanating from its frame captivate me, and I can't help but wonder how all those people fit inside a slender box. I've always been on the thinner side, but there's no way I could squeeze myself into that narrow space. I might try if there was a treat hidden inside, but even I know that would go against the laws of nature.

I tilt my head and raise my eyebrows, studying the people on the screen. One moment, they're laughing and smiling at each other; the next, they're running away with terrified expressions on their faces. My heart starts to pound as I struggle to make sense of what's happening. I don't recognize these people, and their voices grow louder and sharper, which is alarming. I can't tell if they're in danger, but I wonder if they need my help.

As I consider my options, the image changes again, and suddenly the danger has passed. The voices calm down, and I blink rapidly, wondering what I missed and how they escaped their pursuer. The action moves so quickly that I can't keep up. The scenes shift to different locations and feature unfamiliar people in rapid succession. Wait, how did they end up in a car? The whole situation defies everything I understand about the world.

To get into a car, you're supposed to walk outside, open the door, and climb in, but I didn't see any of that happen. One moment, the people were inside an apartment, and the next, they were already driving down the street. The whole sequence is very troubling, and I wonder if some humans have superpowers that allow them to alter space and time. I lower my head to my paws and sigh, and my empty stomach just makes matters worse.

My tummy growls, and I lick my lips, eager to eat the lunch Dad will be serving. He's in charge of preparing our midday meal, and the sunshine streaming through the window tells me it's about that time. I avert my eyes from the screen and try to put the magical people out of my mind. I glance at Dad expectantly and shake my head vigorously, my floppy ears whipping around and smacking the sides of my head. It catches his attention, and I open my mouth to pant at him. He scoots toward me on the couch and pats me affectionately, and I reward him with a slobbery kiss he clearly wasn't expecting. He scrunches his face and wipes the drool from his cheek.

I shift my gaze to the food bowls, trying to signal that it's time for lunch. However, I don't want to be pushy, so I remind myself to wait patiently. Dad scratches behind my ears, and I lean into him, breathing in his familiar scent. Maybe I don't need lunch after all, just infinite pets and hugs. Then Dad pauses, rises, and plods over to the bag of kibble.

I leap up, scamper over, and wag my tail vigorously, my mouth curling into a gleeful smile. The bag makes a satisfying crinkle noise as Dad reaches in with the designated scoop and roots around at the bottom. I hope we still have food because running out would be a total catastrophe. I have no idea how to restock our supply, but Dad always manages to bring home the bacon, so to speak. He periodically hauls in heavy cardboard boxes filled with sacks of dry food. I love watching the process unfold, and it fills me with a warm and contented feeling.

Dad pours one scoop into each bowl, and Rachel and I rush forward. She plunges her head into one dish with enthusiasm, crunching loudly on the kibble, but I take a moment to sniff mine, savoring the aroma and inspecting it for any signs of spoilage or sloppy preparation. Dad adds water on my kibble, and I stare down at the soupy meal, my mouth beginning to water. However, something doesn't feel right. I can't tell if it's the water level, the width of the bowl, or the distance from the floor, but I can't bring myself to take a bite. I step back, turn to Dad, and look up at him with pleading eyes. Confusion churns inside me as I try to pinpoint the problem, hoping that he can fix it.

Dad gently rubs the top of my head and points at the bowl. I glance at it and then back at him, my face a perfect mix of bewilderment and innocence. He crouches and taps the side of the bowl lightly, but I only stare at it forlornly. I can't quite put my paw on it, and the food still doesn't look appealing. I remain skeptical and give the bowl a long sniff. The delicious scent of sweet potato, one of my favorite flavors, reaches my nose. My mouth falls open, and drool drips down my long tongue.

I glance over at Rachel, who is greedily chowing down on the kibble. She accidentally drops a piece on the floor and lunges forward to snatch it before it rolls away. I admire her focus and speed. She excels at making meals disappear in record time, and if I don't start working on my lunch, then it'll soon draw her attention. I'm slightly worried about it, and I raise my eyebrows at Dad.

He lifts the bowl to my nose. I sniff eagerly but still refuse to eat. Dad sighs, murmurs my name, and plunges his hand into the soupy mix. Holding a handful to my mouth, he lets the kibble-flavored liquid drip back into the bowl. I hesitate before licking the food from his palm. Dad grabs another handful and offers it to me. This time, I dive in immediately, gobbling it up and savoring the flavors as I lick his fingers. We repeat the process, slowly emptying the bowl and leaving a huge mess on the floor.

Rachel polishes off her meal and assesses my remaining kibble. Dad positions himself between us, and she steps forward to peer over his shoulder, watching the process with interest. I hope she doesn't muscle in on my mealtime just because she's the faster eater. I can't have her disrupting my loving moment with Dad.

I accelerate my pace, gulping down handfuls of the mushy food as fast as Dad can supply them. When I've consumed every piece, I stare down at the brown water in the bowl. It might be appetizing, but it's not in Dad's hand, so I'm unsure if I want it.

Dad climbs to his feet, wanders into the kitchen, and turns on the sink. He washes his hands multiple times a day, which feels like far too much bathing for my taste. While I watch him, Rachel rushes over and greedily drinks the remaining kibble water. I watch with dismay, realizing I did want Dad to hand it to me. Rachel licks the dish clean and stares down at it longingly. We both hate when the food is gone.

Dad strolls over and rubs a small towel across the floor, replacing the bowl in its original position and removing all traces of the spilled liquid. My stomach is full, and I feel satiated after the tasty meal. Suddenly, I open my mouth and let out a loud burp in Dad's face. He looks at me for a moment and then bursts into laughter, which warms my heart. He calls my name and sits back on his heels, gently rubbing my neck. I'm very pleased with myself.

Rachel sidles up beside him, and he drops the towel on the floor, using both hands to pet us. I nuzzle his arm, thanking him for the tasty meal and attentive service. I think this should become our normal routine, with him handing me my food, so I don't have to stoop and stick my nose into the frightening bowl. I appreciate everything he does to keep us comfortable and well fed.

There's something alluring and special about food that is served to me, and it seems tastier and more desirable than regular kibble sitting quietly in a designated dish. Hand food is a delicacy, and each morsel I lap from Dad's palm strengthens the connection between us.

Rachel turns and sniffs Dad's hand, no doubt smelling the lingering scent of lunch on his skin. She begins to lick him enthusiastically, savoring the mix of kibble and the citrus soap he uses. Dad laughs again and pulls her into a gentle hug. Rachel stands quietly, enjoying the moment, and glances over at me before tilting her head toward Dad's kibble-scented fingers. I step forward and lick that hand, which is just out of Rachel's reach. There's nothing I love more than our family lunches.

Leslie Popp

## Rachel

### Field Trips and Felines

Today feels like a special day, although I'm not sure why yet. Dad is packing our food and water bowls, tossing a bag of kibble into a suitcase, and tucking my favorite blanket on top. This can only mean one thing—we're going on a road trip! Car rides are the best, and I fully support any outing that involves cruising around town—unless it's a trip to the vet. In that case, I'm completely against it. But since our bowls and blankets never come along for vet visits, we must be heading to another destination.

I watch eagerly as Dad struggles to close the bag, tucking in the edge of the blanket before zipping it shut with a satisfying *zzzzt* sound. Then he grabs our leashes, and Sara and I rush forward, bouncing with excitement. We're going outside! I stare at the door, wishing Dad had tied his shoes before clipping on my leash. Now we have to wait while he tightens his shoelaces and gives each one a final tug.

Finally, we set off on our adventure, pulling the suitcase along behind us. To my delight, an unfamiliar vehicle is parked at the curb, and Dad helps us into the backseat, making sure our leashes don't get caught in the door. I'm bursting with excitement, tail wagging uncontrollably. I press my nose against the window, thrilled to be a dog in a car instead of a dog stuck at home. It's a major upgrade from our usual walks and the best way to tour the city.

The vehicle rumbles to life, and we're soon cruising along at an impressive speed. My tongue falls out of my mouth, and I pant with excitement as I enjoy the ride through the neighborhood. Soon, we enter unfamiliar territory, and I watch strangers hurrying down the sidewalk. Cars zoom past, and we stop at a multicolored light. I observe people pass quickly in front of our vehicle, and when the light changes, we're off again.

I sniff the city air, which smells of gasoline and pizza, and it fills me with a comforting sense of normalcy. It's my city, which means every crumb of pizza should be mine. I haven't figured out how to make that happen yet, but trust me, I'm working on it. I nod at the pedestrians and give them a friendly grin, showing off my impeccable dog manners.

"I can't stop and chat with you, but you seem nice!" I call out to a couple walking with a small white dog. "To pet me, look for me on patrol. I live up the street, so come by any time!"

I wag my tail with delight, hoping they'll visit me soon. Meeting new dogs is still a challenge, but I try to remain calm and trust that they mean no harm. I'm working on a new me, and practice makes perfect. We pause at another light, and I spot a man in a fancy suit walking briskly while eating a folded piece of pizza. My mouth waters instantly, and I wonder if he might be generous enough to share a bite.

I press my face to the glass, willing him to slide the savory slice through the window and into my open mouth. But he turns the corner, taking his lunch with him.

I see a dog staring back at me from another car and watch nervously as it barks. I can't tell if it's happy or defensive barking, but the windows give me a sense of safety. A few minutes later, a vehicle with a fluffy golden face hanging out the back window pulls up alongside us. This dog reminds me of Sara, and I immediately perk up, plastering a friendly expression on my face. The newcomer gazes at me and wags its tail, and I wish I could hop into the other car to say hello. I'm sure the human behind the wheel is kind and generously hands out head scratches. However, no time to linger as we zip down the street.

"See you later!" I shout, hoping that the dog can hear me. Perhaps we'll run into each other on the sidewalk and become playmates at the dog run.

Finally, the vehicle comes to a stop in front of a tall building, and Dad helps us out of the car, gently lifting Sara so she doesn't strain her disabled leg. A familiar scent greets my nose. MOM! I bounce up and down, scanning the area for Mom, but all I see are unfamiliar faces. Her smell is stronger by the door, and I dart inside as Dad yanks it open. He struggles with the suitcase, and I feel guilty for dragging him along, but Mom is in this building, and I'm anxious to see her. We take a short ride in the elevator and are led down a narrow hallway to an apartment door. My nose is drawn to her scent, and I can barely contain my excitement because this must be where she lives when she's not at home with us. I think back to the car ride and wish that I had paid closer attention to the turns we made, but I didn't understand the importance of our outing today. I should have created a detailed mental map of the route so I can visit Mom anytime.

She opens the door and smiles broadly, making me feel all gooey inside, before stepping back and welcoming us to her home. Sara charges through the door, and I follow suit, bouncing lightly on my feet and snorting excitedly while vigorously wagging my tail.

"We found you!" I announce, grinning up at her and letting my tongue hang out. "I knew we would eventually discover where you live! I would like to move in so we can be together every day."

I sit at her feet and stare into her big brown eyes, wondering if my heart could be any fuller. Dad embraces her lovingly, and Sara licks her leg, leaving a wet smudge behind.

After the initial excitement, I scan my surroundings and freeze in horror when a pair of yellow eyes locks onto me. Fearing for my life, I feel completely unprepared for a confrontation. The eyes are attached to a large orange cat sporting an elegant pattern of stripes. He's perched atop a tower equipped with a cozy looking cradle and is staring down at me intently, flicking his tail in irritation. He holds his head high and sits with his paws turned out, giving him a sophisticated and regal air. The cat doesn't speak and continues to glare at me.

I drop my gaze to the floor and hold perfectly still, hoping that I haven't been seen, even though I know the yellow eyes are on me. Confused and uncertain, I let my head hang low and study the swirling patterns of the hardwood flooring. I muster up some courage, take a deep breath, and hope that when I look up the cat will be gone, proving to be only a figment of my imagination. To my dismay, the orange ruler of the house still watches me with unblinking eyes. I avert my gaze, wishing that I could disappear and escape the scrutiny of this strange feline.

Sara is completely unaware of the four-legged resident in the tower and is sniffing along the floorboards, exploring every inch of the hallway before entering the next room. She wags her tail and accidentally knocks several shoes off the low shelf by the door. The noise startles her, and she looks over her shoulder in confusion. It doesn't bother her for long, and she continues to explore the apartment.

Sara lifts her head and spots the cat, who is intently observing her behavior. She opens her mouth in a goofy grin and greets him with a friendly wag. He remains stoic, failing to reciprocate the greeting, and gives her an irritated look that says, "What are you doing in my house?"

I begin to shake, worrying that the cat is about to strike. I have to protect my sister, and I'm determined to intervene, but terror grips my heart. I stand helplessly in the entryway and stare at the ground, hoping for the best.

Mom breaks the tension by gently patting my head, strolling over to the commanding feline, and extending that hand for his inspection. He leans forward and takes a tentative sniff, glancing at me and then at Sara. Mom lovingly strokes his head and back, and he relaxes at her touch. He rubs his head against her palm and closes his eyes for a moment, enjoying the attention. When he opens them again, his demeanor is calmer, but I still find him unsettling and creepy.

I feel like an intruder in this house, and I hope that he'll allow me to stay. I take a small step forward, keeping my head low so the cat understands that I respect his territory and mean no harm. Sara continues to pant softly and watch him with curiosity. She wants to approach him and sniff his fur but is restraining herself, given his standoffish behavior.

Mom returns to my side, and Dad gives me a gentle push, wanting me to proceed into the main room. I oblige and take several fearful steps, shaking with anxiety. The orange feline is still tracking me with those piercing eyes that seem to look right through me.

"Pumpkin, do you want to say hi?" Mom asks in a soothing voice. "Come here, Pumpkin."

She's asking the cat to introduce himself, and I conclude that his name must be Pumpkin. He ignores her question and sits quietly, flicking his tail from side to side. I wish that I knew what he was thinking, but he cleverly conceals his emotions and assesses the situation with those steely eyes. Sara's tail swishes happily, and I try to focus on her instead. She isn't bothered by Pumpkin's cold reception and is intent on befriending the owner of this residence, which I now understand is the cat, not Mom.

"Excuse me, sir," I murmur under my breath. "It's very nice to meet you."

I always remain polite, hoping that good manners and a friendly greeting will win anyone over. I keep my distance, standing behind Sara to be safe. Mom acts as an ambassador, familiarizing Pumpkin with my scent and trying to convince him to accept me into the household. My chest tightens as I worry he might reject me and force me to leave.

Dad puts bowls of food and water out for us and spreads the blanket on the floor. Sara immediately sprawls out, making herself comfortable. The cat will pass judgement in time, and Sara isn't going to worry about it. I lie down by her side, unable to relax.

Dad rubs my back and speaks softly, reassuring me that I'm welcome here and everything will be alright. I take several deep breaths to calm my nerves and remind myself that Dad has the situation under control and that this prowling feline is not a threat. Minutes tick by, and I continue to imagine worst-case scenarios. I keep glancing over at Pumpkin, whose intense gaze is unnerving.

Suddenly, I hear a soft thump and sense a faint vibration through the floorboards. The hair on the back of my neck rises, and every sense warns me that someone is approaching. Panic wells up inside me, and I wish that I had positioned myself to face Pumpkin's tower so I would see him coming.

Sara's tail begins to wag again, and I know that he's busy assessing us and pacing around the blanket. I hold my breath and try not to startle him. I want Pumpkin to accept me and conclude that I would be a valued member of this household. He maintains his distance but looks at me with curiosity, which seems like a positive sign. I keep my head down and let my ears tilt forward to show that I'm friendly. He sniffs the air and inspects me thoroughly. Our eyes meet, and he quickly turns and struts into the bedroom, hopping onto the bed and snuggling into the fuzzy blanket. I've

## The Bark Diaries

dreamed of sleeping on a human bed, and I'm temporarily distracted by the revelation that this one is low to the ground, making it easy for me to hoist myself onto its plush surface.

I feel more at ease and assume I've passed the initial inspection. The cat appears skeptical but makes no move to intimidate me or persuade Mom to turn against me. I lower my head to my paws and drift into a brief nap, exhausted from the excitement of the car ride and the challenge of meeting our new feline acquaintance. I think our first encounter went well, though a heads-up next time would help me prepare myself.

Leslie Popp

## Rachel

## Bath Time

Apparently, retrievers are supposed to love water, but I'm a retriever mix, and whatever I'm mixed with clearly despises it. I have a strong aversion to wet fur and loathe bath time.

Mom and Dad, on the other hand, seem to enjoy getting wet. They voluntarily climb into the tub to play in the water. They don't have much fur, just a patch on the tops of their heads, so I'm not sure why they need to wash it so often. When Mom finally emerges, she smells like flowers and releases a cloud of warm steam as she opens the bathroom door. I'm relieved she survived another encounter with water. She's clearly more experienced with baths than I am, and while I have faith in her judgment, I still get nervous every time she disappears behind that curtain.

I don't ever need a bath. My smell is perfectly dog-like, natural, familiar, and just as it should be. I steer clear of mud and only step in puddles whenever necessary. I keep my paws clean with regular licking, and Mom brushes my thick coat to remove loose fur and any debris from our outdoor adventures. Between the two of us, we maintain an effective hygiene routine without resorting to soap and water. Problem solved!

Baths are unpredictable, and today I sense something suspicious. Mom has gathered a stack of towels, and Dad is clearing away the numerous bottles crowding the edge of the tub and removing the cushioned mats from the floor. Their behavior is unsettling, so I lower my head and remain quiet, hoping they'll forget that I'm here. Maybe they're just tidying up, and it has nothing to do with me. Not everything revolves around me, after all. I've seen them scour the tub with foul-smelling liquids before, and it seems like one of those days—except my nose doesn't detect any of the usual cleaning odors. For once, I wish I did. I sigh, raise my eyebrows, and glance around warily keeping my eyes trained on the bathroom. Sara sleeps soundly through it all, unfazed by the looming threat of water. I envy her calm and confidence; I don't know what I would do without my big sister.

Dad strolls over to me, sporting red shorts and no shirt, which is another troubling sign, since I tend to send water flying in all directions during a bath. He has a special water-friendly outfit reserved for this task. I hold perfectly still, hoping he intends to bathe only Sara. Her shaggy fur traps dirt, and her breath could use a mint, so she is the more likely candidate. My hygiene, on the other hand, is impeccable, and I see no reason to participate.

Dad pats his legs and calls my name, urging me to come closer, but I feign confusion and stay put. When he slides his arms beneath my belly to lift me, I spring to my feet in protest. Being carried is undignified; a proper dog should keep all four paws firmly on the ground. Despite my resistance, he guides me toward the bathroom, and I quickly realize my mistake in cooperating. I pause at the doorway, refusing to go further, then bolt in the opposite direction. Dad anticipates the escape attempt and catches me mid-stride, cradling me firmly before depositing me in the white tub. He strokes my head reassuringly as Mom closes the door to prevent my escape. I test my luck by trying to hop out of the tub, but she blocks my exit and distracts me with gentle scratches behind my ears, which is a tactic that leaves me torn between enjoying her affection and fleeing from the inevitable bath.

Suddenly, warm water begins streaming down from a metal showerhead attached to a flexible hose. It's normally mounted on the wall where it spews artificial rain, but it can be detached for use in close quarters. I shiver as the toasty water peppers my back and soaks my lovely coat. My reaction has little to do with the water temperature and everything to do with my anxiety. I gaze up at Mom, willing her to help me escape, but she just smiles, says my name softly, and rubs my neck reassuringly.

Dad massages the oatmeal shampoo into my fur, causing it to stick up at odd angles, before drenching me again and diligently rinsing out the suds. I lean my body into Mom, soaking her legs and dripping water all over the floor as I stick my head out of the tub. A puddle forms on the tile, which is nothing compared to the torrent raining down in the white basin that I'm trapped in.

## The Bark Diaries

I try to think happy thoughts about walks in the sunshine, treats, snuggling on the couch, and finding food on the floor. However, I can't ignore the soggy feel of my fur and the steady rain peppering my back and sides. I'm inconsolable and shake violently while Mom attempts to soothe me. I want to return to my cozy spot on the floor. I'd even be willing to promise that I'll never get dirty again and will diligently lick my paws twice a day. I'll wear little booties outside if it means that I can avoid future baths.

Dad washes my ears and sloshes water on my chest. I lift my head to direct the torrent away from my face, but he pours more on my neck, and it begins dripping down my cheeks. I hope this troublesome event will be over soon.

"I'm clean now," I announce shakily. "I think we're done here."

I close my eyes and wait, anticipating what will happen next. To my delight, the waterfall ceases, and I pause, watching warily to see if it will start again. Dad steps out of the tub, and I exhale a long, relieved sigh. His exit signals the end of the washing stage and the beginning of the drying stage. I close my eyes, brace myself, and give a vigorous shake, sending droplets flying in every direction. Mom scrambles to close the shower curtain to stop the water from drenching the room, but my head still protrudes from the tub, blocking her path. Now she's soaked, and I can't help feeling a sense of satisfaction that none of us escaped unscathed. My fur is pointing in every direction and will need to be styled, but I feel incredibly pleased with my performance.

Mom steps back, and I hop out of the tub, preparing to shake again. A towel is thrown over me before I can cast off the residual water, and Dad rubs me down, pressing the towel to my ears to absorb the liquid. I appreciate his efforts and immediately forgive him for bathing me in the first place. I feel bedraggled and stare down at the floor, shivering from the stressful ordeal.

The room erupts with a roaring sound, and I step back, startled. Mom waves a handheld dryer, blowing warm air across my fur. We've performed this routine before, but the noise is unsettling, and the heat quickly becomes overwhelming. I crouch low and pant softly, hoping my fur will dry without further assistance from the screeching device. After a few minutes, Dad applies another towel to my back and gives me a vigorous massage. I shake again, but this time nothing flies off.

The floor is wet, and covered in a layer of fur, yet I feel fluffy and soft, and I smell clean and fresh. I'm proud of facing my fear and adding another bath to my list of heroic accomplishments.

Mom opens the door, and I scamper out, eager to put some distance between myself and the memories of the tub and dryer. The experience is jarring, but at least the next bath won't come for many weeks, so I can relax and enjoy a peaceful reprieve.

Trotting into the living room, I flop down beside Sara, worn out from the ordeal. I sniff my paws and lick away a bit of water from between my toes. Sara glances at me, sniffs my neck, and casts a wary look toward the bathroom, where a cleanup operation is underway. I can see the alarm in her eyes, as she realizes that her turn is approaching.

## The Bark Diaries

Mom wanders over and begins brushing me, running the comb through my thick fur. Mom's voice is reassuring, and the undivided attention makes me feel closer to her. We're just two girls doing our hair and sharing secrets.

"I don't like the bath," I think to myself.

"Good girl," she says. "You did so well. I know you don't like the bath, but you were such a trooper. What a good girl you are."

My eyes grow wide, and I gaze at her in wonder. Does she understand me? Can she hear my thoughts? I tilt my head to one side and then the other, contemplating the question. I've never considered this possibility before, and it could be a coincidence, but I believe that Mom is a mind reader. That's amazing!

"I want treats," I think excitedly. "Two treats—no, all the treats!"

"Good girl," she repeats.

I wag my tail at being called a good girl because that's my number one goal in life. My bravery in the bath has clearly pleased Mom, and I can't help feeling proud, despite the lingering dampness between my toes. I want Mom and Dad to be proud of me, but I also want those treats. Mom is either declining my request or pretending not to hear it, but now that I know she can read minds, I'll think about treats whenever she's nearby. Honestly, I daydream about snacks most of the time anyway, so thinking about food won't be difficult. A piece of bread with peanut butter or one of those bone-shaped biscuits would do nicely. My stomach rumbles as I consider the possibilities.

*Sara*

# Vanilla Cupcakes

A clatter and bang from the kitchen jolts me awake from my afternoon nap. I pry my eyes open, sleep still clinging heavily to my eyelids, and survey the room for intruders. I was enjoying a lovely dream about finally catching that pesky pigeon in the park. The memory fills me with a sense of pride, even if it was only a dream. After all, we should always take a moment to appreciate our accomplishments.

I hear drawers and cabinets opening and closing, so I sit up, shake my head to clear the remnants of sleep, and focus my senses. Something unusual is happening, and I need to investigate the disturbance. I spot Mom in the kitchen, moving from one cabinet to another as she searches through the well-stocked shelves. I roll onto my stomach, stretch my stiff muscles, and trot over to see what she's doing.

Mom crouches in front of a low cabinet, removes an assortment of containers and paper bags, and places them neatly on the counter. I stand beside her, peer into the dark cupboard, and marvel at the abundance of food inside. My mouth waters as I imagine her preparing a delicious meal for us. If she's cooking dinner, I hope she remembers to fill my bowl with a savory treat. I lean closer and press my nose against her cheek, breaking her concentration. She startles, loses her balance, and lands gently on her backside, still clutching a white container in one hand. Blinking in surprise, she pats my head with a laugh and climbs back to her feet.

"I'm here to assist with dinner preparations," I announce, wagging my tail and gazing up at her expectantly. "I would like to apply for the position of official taste tester. What can I sample first?"

Mom gathers an assortment of bowls, spoons, and small cups then retrieves a glass container marked with lines along its side. She steps back to take an inventory of the collection and gives a satisfied nod of approval. I nod too, eager to show my support and get involved in this important operation. Everything appears to be in order.

Mom steps around me, opens the chilly box that humans call the refrigerator, and rummages through its contents. She adds another item to her growing pile, nods again, and I faithfully mimic her every move.

Then the real work begins, and I watch intently as she retrieves a metal tray with circular troughs and drops a thin paper liner into each one. My ears perk up, and a wave of giddy anticipation courses through me as I recognize those liners. We're making cupcakes!

Let me explain something—I adore cupcakes. I love their sweet aroma, the creamy frosting, the sponge-like texture, and the simple joy they inspire in everyone around them. Cupcakes are tiny parcels of happiness, each one capable of brightening even the gloomiest day. Have you ever seen someone frown while eating a cupcake? Of course not. That's because cupcakes are pure magic. Honestly, try to name something better than a cupcake—you can't.

Since we've established that cupcakes are in the works, I'm very motivated to assist Mom and speed things along. I plant myself at her side, lean gently against her leg, and repeat my generous offer to help.

Mom taps the stove a few times, and it responds with a series of beeps. I hear it hum to life, and a light flickers inside. I press my nose to the glass, but there's nothing to see in there—yet. Soon, this magical machine will transform cake batter into fluffy little cakes, filling the house with their irresistible aroma.

Mom begins measuring the ingredients, sending a small plume of white dust into the air as she dumps several cups of the bland powder into the bowl. I make a mental note: step one, add white powder. Next, she digs into a bag of pearly granules that smell sweet and inviting, scoops out a precise amount, and adds it to the mixture. A few more powders are added, and then she stirs everything together, transforming a jumble of ingredients into the promise of delicious cupcakes.

I lick her leg, wanting to reward her hard work and express my deep affection. She tastes like flowery lotion, and I work my way down to her knee, savoring the flavor on my tongue. Mom says my name, and I look up. She steps to the side and shifts the bowl along the counter. She's out of my licking range, but I think she understood my message.

Mom then pours cloudy liquid into the glass container with the markings down the side, stooping to check that it's filled to the correct level before layering on an oily substance and adding the liquid ingredients to the dry mixture. She opens a small bottle with a white flower on the label and shakes a few aromatic drops into the mixture before vigorously stirring the contents together. She holds the bowl firmly as she combines the powders and liquids into a smooth and silky potion. Turning to the metal tray waiting patiently by her side, Mom spoons in the tasty concoction, being careful not to spill the precious ingredients.

I plant a joyful lick on the back of her knee, and she lets out a soft giggle as she inches away from my slobbery tongue. We shift further down the counter, but I don't mind. These little cakes are a delicacy, and if we need to use every inch of kitchen space to craft them, then that's what we'll do. We can slide along the length of the counter until we reach the end if that's a necessary part of the process.

Mom inserts the metal tray into the oven, closes the hinged door, and presses a few buttons. Then she turns and kisses the top of my head, and I try to lick her face. She anticipates this move and keeps her rosy cheeks just out of my reach. I lower my head and run my tongue across her ankle instead, wiggling my butt and wagging my tail happily. She makes a gentle cooing noise and giggles.

Mom begins to tidy up the kitchen, scrubbing bowls and utensils and replacing the ingredients in the respective cabinets and drawers. I remain by her side, periodically glancing over my shoulder at the oven in case the cupcakes come tumbling out and land on the floor. A dog can only dream of such a glorious accident.

## Leslie Popp

The room fills with a sugary aroma that makes my nose twitch in delight. My mouth waters as I think about the spongy cakes, and I run my tongue across my lips to keep from drooling on the floor. I bet I could scarf down those sweet treats in under a minute. Perhaps that's ambitious, but I would certainly try. At the very least, I could lick each one so no one else would eat them.

Suddenly, Mom pulls out a hand-held machine with two spinning arms that twirl with purpose. She retrieves a yellow block that smells of fat and salt and drops it into the clean bowl. The machine whips the block into a fluffy cream, and I watch the arms whirl rhythmically, their motion almost hypnotic. Mom sprinkles in some sweet granules and adds a dash of brown liquid from the bottle with the white flower—surely the secret ingredient. The metal arms resume their spinning until the mixture is light and airy. I give Mom's knee a grateful lick in approval.

The oven emits a high-pitched beeping sound that hurts my sensitive ears. Luckily, Mom administers a firm tap, and it ceases the offending tone. I sigh in relief and tilt my head at the machine in disapproval. Mom slips a thick glove onto her hand and removes the metal tray, which is brimming with fluffy cupcakes. I track her movements, unwilling to blink and let the cakes out of my sight. She sets them on top of the stove, carefully removes the tiny treats from their individual troughs, and places them on the counter. Steam rises from their golden domes, and while I know they're hot, I would still swallow one whole if given the opportunity.

We begin the painstaking process of waiting for them to cool, which seems to take forever. Mom wanders off to handle another task, but I maintain a sentry position, not wanting the cupcakes to roll away or for someone else to sample one before me. I don't have any plans this afternoon, and this responsibility is my top priority. I'm thrilled to help Mom by guarding our treasured baked goods. I'm such a faithful dog and an excellent helper. No one is more attentive and focused than me when it comes to cupcakes.

By the time Mom strolls back into the room, I'm impatient, but I try to remain calm. She touches the top of one domed treat, nods in satisfaction, and begins to spread the creamy frosting onto the cake. She takes great care with each one, making sure they look as good as I'm sure they taste. Soon there's a row of white-capped desserts on the counter, and I scoot forward and press my nose against her thigh in case she forgot that I'm waiting.

Before we can eat, Mom insists on tidying up again, and I have to endure the long minutes as she scrubs the kitchen. Once the counters are clean and the bowl and metal tray sit drying beside the sink, Mom finally turns her attention back to me.

Suddenly, Dad strides into the room and makes a beeline for my cupcakes. I give him a pleading look, and he scratches behind my ears, which I appreciate. He says a few words to Mom and points to the sweet treats. She murmurs something that sounds like "vanilla cupcakes," and my eyes grow wide. Finally, I have a name for these tasty delights wrapped in thin paper packages. I've always just called them cupcakes, mini sweet treats, tiny spongy wonders, sugar-kissed cakes, and bite-sized delights. Vanilla sounds exotic, and I repeat it several times in my head so I don't forget.

Vanilla cupcakes are even more delightful than plain cupcakes.

Dad grabs the largest cupcake and shoves it into his mouth, finishing it in just a few bites. I feel a pang of jealousy and shift anxiously from paw to paw, hoping that he won't eat them all before I get my turn. I haven't fulfilled my taste tester duties yet. Stepping forward, I position myself between Mom and Dad, giving them my most pleading, wide-eyed stare.

"Don't forget that I helped," I remind them. "I would appreciate a snack. I promise it won't spoil my appetite."

Mom selects another cupcake, removes the paper liner, and crouches beside me. She divides the little cake into four pieces and holds one out to me in the palm of her hand. I wag my tail and lunge forward, devouring the sweet morsel in one triumphant gulp. She offers me the remaining three pieces, waiting for me to swallow each one before presenting me with the next, which slows down the process. Once I've erased all traces of the sugary dream cake—I mean—vanilla cupcake, I stare down at Mom's empty hand, hoping that another cupcake will materialize. Unfortunately, Mom transfers the rest of them into a sealed container on the counter that's out of my reach.

With my stomach full and energy renewed, I spend the afternoon following Mom and Dad around the house and resting my head on their knees whenever they sit. I replay the cupcake recipe in my mind again and again, determined not to forget a single step. It goes something like this.

The Bark Diaries

## **<u>Sara's Vanilla Cupcake Recipe</u>**

- Gather a bowl, cups, and utensils.
- Place paper liners into the metal tray.
- Turn on the stove by pressing a few buttons (Warning: It will beep!).
- Pour several cups of white powder, a cup of sweet-smelling granules, and small spoonfuls of the other magical powders into the bowl.
- Mix everything together thoroughly.
- Add a glass of creamy liquid, a smaller portion of the oily substance, and a spoonful of the fragrant liquid from the bottle with the white flower (Note: This is probably the secret ingredient).
- Stir the mixture until smooth, then fill the lined tray compartments with the batter.
- Insert the tray into the oven, close the door, and press a few more buttons (Warning: More beeps!).
- Wait patiently for the timer to go off before removing the cupcakes and letting them cool—or eat them while they're still warm if you can't resist.
- Make the creamy topping by placing the yellow block of fat in a clean bowl and whipping it with the spinning machine until smooth.
- Add a cup of sweet powder and a few drops from the flowery bottle.
- Let the machine spin until the mixture is fluffy and spreadable.
- Spoon the sweet topping onto the cooled cupcakes.

- Eat immediately (share if you like, or hoard them all for yourself).

## Rachel

### Dancing and Kisses

I spend most days observing Mom and Dad and occasionally joining their activities. Their behavior is endlessly amusing, and I patiently wait for a passing head pat or kind word.

With a flexible schedule, I can easily change my plans to make time for family gatherings. Just the other day, I rescheduled my afternoon nap to follow Mom around while she cleaned the apartment. I panted enthusiastically by her side as she expertly wiped surfaces with pungent liquids until they were shiny. She organized the kitchen, scrubbed the counters, straightened my food and water bowls, and wiped away the spill I'd made earlier after drinking and leaving a trail of droplets across the floor. I tried not to look guilty when she mopped up my mess, hoping that she would blame someone else for it.

I enjoy participating in family tasks, as long as I can stay close to Mom or Dad. As a loyal helper, I'm content to observe quietly and offer an encouraging wag of my tail every now and then. Human behavior never fails to intrigue me, and I lend a paw whenever possible. After all, it's my house too, and I like seeing everything clean and organized. My paws lack the dexterity of Mom's hands, but I can still be her cheerleader while she completes the tougher chores. I shower her with approving looks to show my gratitude for her hard work. Whether helping her directly or simply keeping her company, I'm always eager to be part of the day's work.

"You're doing an excellent job at yoga today! I think you're a natural," I call enthusiastically while pacing around and wagging my tail vigorously. "The floor is sparkling after you cleaned it this morning, and it smells fresh too!"

See, I'm an expert at being supportive, regardless of the activity or my level of involvement. Mom and Dad appreciate my company and reward me with hugs and back rubs. What would I do without them?

Today, Mom listens to music while brushing her hair and applying creams and powders to her face. I love the way she looks, regardless of her hairstyle, the color of her eyelids, and the clothes she's wearing. Yoga pants, a cotton t-shirt, and natural-colored eyelids are a sign that she's going to stay home with me, and I prefer those days when we can just snuggle on the couch.

I don't understand all the words of the song, but I enjoy the rhythm, and it makes Mom smile, so it has become my new favorite tune. I pant to the beat, hoping that it'll mention walks, treats, back rubs, or chasing pigeons, which are the best things in life. I listen for these key terms, my tail twitching as soon as I hear the first keyword.

## The Bark Diaries

Mom shakes her hips in time to the beat, hums softly, and breaks into song. Her voice is unmistakable, and I would recognize it anywhere. I close my eyes and feel the music pulse through me from the tip of my snout to my tailbone.

Mom strolls out of the bathroom and sees me lounging in the hallway, waiting patiently for her to finish her morning routine. I'm excited to have her full attention, especially when she kneels and massages my neck in time to the music. I could certainly get used to such pampering and would happily clear my morning schedule.

A new song begins, and Mom dances around the room, her feet bouncing with the beat and her arms and hips swaying gracefully. I spring to my paws, matching her enthusiasm, and bound from one side of her to the other. She reaches out without missing a beat, and I press my wet nose to her palm before spinning in a tight circle and wagging so vigorously that my whole body shakes. I let my mouth hang open and pant as we move together. I don't have many moves, but I nail the tight circle, graceful bound, and wild wag with surprising skill. I'm light on my feet and savor every playful second with Mom.

Mom scratches the itchy spot on my lower back, and I accidentally "back that thang up" right into her leg, stepping on her foot. Startled by my rookie mistake, I spring away. Stepping on your partner's foot is never ideal, but it happens to me occasionally. Mom just laughs, and the sound fills my chest with warmth. It's a reminder of how much she adores me. I'm grateful that she overlooks my clumsiness and never makes me feel self-conscious. Mistakes always worry me, but stepping on her foot feels like a minor offense.

## Leslie Popp

We continue our coordinated dance until the song ends, and I'm breathing heavily from the exertion. I probably need more exercise to build stamina, since a single dance shouldn't leave me this breathless, although the apartment is a bit warm with my thick coat. I remind myself that it's just my fluffy fur making the activity more difficult, and I feel better about it.

Mom kneels beside me, wraps her arms around my neck, and plants a kiss on the top of my head. I continue panting and wagging, and I'm content to enjoy the affection all day. She pulls back, but I scoot closer and lean in for another hug. Mom massages my back and beams at me, and I let my mouth fall open in a grin, showing her just how much she means to me. She's my favorite person, and I want to spend every moment by her side.

Sara watches the activity from the couch, her favorite spot in the room. She's excited, but her limp prevents her from joining in the fun. I can tell she imagines herself bounding around the room alongside me. Mom hurries over, takes Sara's thin face in her hands, and plants gentle kisses on her brow so she doesn't feel left out. Sara tries to return the favor with a sloppy lick, but Mom skillfully avoids it and scratches behind her ears instead.

Mom collapses on the couch beside Sara, who immediately rolls over, rests her head on her lap, and is rewarded with a belly rub and soft praise. I want to participate in this family moment, so I hop onto the other cushion, scoot close to Mom, and pant in her face so she doesn't forget about me. Sara rolls onto her back to allow for easier belly rub access. Her gangly legs stick up awkwardly, but she doesn't care and looks incredibly pleased with her current position. If Mom stops petting her, she'll wiggle around furiously, flailing all four legs until Mom resumes the activity.

I'm not an aggressive licker. In fact, I try to give anyone I lick a chance to move away or lean in for a hug. I inch closer to Mom and lift my eyebrows to get her attention. She smiles, and I wag my tail as she rubs my neck. I step closer to her so she can feel my warm breath on her shoulder. She remains still, so I lean forward, pausing an inch from her cheek to make sure she's comfortable with my proximity. Then I give her a gentle lick—a quick, careful peck, not a sloppy kiss—to show that I love her even more than treats.

Mom laughs and pulls me into a warm hug. Sara wiggles excitedly on the floor, begging for more belly rubs. I watch the playful chaos over Mom's shoulder, feeling safe in her embrace. I lean forward and sniff her hair and neck, taking in the familiar scent. Mom leans back and kisses my cheek, which makes me feel shy. She then pets Sara with one hand while gently patting my head with the other. I close my eyes, savoring this perfect family moment. Our first dance ends with a tender kiss.

# Leslie Popp

## *Sara*

### Chariot Ride

Mom is sitting on the couch with her bare feet dangling over the edge. Her little toes are practically begging to be sniffed. I stretch out on the floor and study her face, examining the gentle curve of her nose, her dark brown eyes, and the rosy hue of her cheeks. She's my favorite person in the world, and I make it my mission to keep her in sight at all times. She rarely stays still, drifting from room to room and giving me quite the workout as I trail behind her. I don't mind the exercise, but my favorite part of the day is when she finally settles on the couch, so I can stretch out beside her while she watches TV. When she gets up, she has to step over me, and I'm usually rewarded with a gentle head pat.

    I lean forward and sniff her toes, breathing in the unique scent of her feet. They smell like soap from the shower, but no amount of scrubbing can remove the underlying aroma of deliciously sweaty feet. Flowery soap and warm water can't hide her true smell from my nose. I brush my whiskers against her little toe by mistake, and she giggles, quickly sliding her foot away. I wag my tail in response to the joyful noise and gaze up at her smiling face. I scoot forward, sniff the length of that foot, and lick her heel. She says my name, but I'm distracted by the alluring taste, running my slobbery tongue over her arch and toes before pausing for another sniff. Then I start over again, beginning with the heel and ending with the smallest toe.

She shifts her weight and tucks her feet beneath the blanket, just out of my reach. I'm puzzled—why would she hide them in the middle of such a beautiful moment? I haven't had the opportunity to attend to her other foot, and the imbalance troubles me. I'll stay alert and sneak a quick lick whenever she becomes distracted.

The sound of the front door opening draws my attention, and I turn my ears in that direction. I hear a box being dragged across the floor, and then Dad comes into view, lugging the oversized package into the living room. I tilt my head, curious about what present we've received. I love surprises.

Dad opens the cardboard box and produces a large cushion covered in a fluffy material. He drops it on the floor, kneels, and presses his palms into the soft surface, assessing whether it's up to his standards. The fuzzy material springs back when he removes his hands, and I wonder what he plans to do with this thing. It's too small to cover the bed and too large to fit on the couch.

Dad slides the cushion across the floor, positions it by my side, and glances at me. I stare back at him, wondering what he expects me to do with it. He points to the cushion, and I examine it for a moment before returning my attention to his face. He's beaming and again points to the new furniture, gently patting it with his hand and beckoning to me. I consider the situation, rise to my feet, and thoroughly sniff the fuzzy pillow. It carries the scent of the box, the soft foam inside, and the crisp, fresh cloth. As far as I can tell, it hasn't been claimed by another animal.

Suddenly, it dawns on me. I step onto the plush cushion, sinking into the spongy material, and Dad smiles. I turn in a circle, searching for the perfect spot and loving the feel of it beneath my paws. Then I flop down and bury my face in the fabric. Dad says my name and kisses the top of my head. I've been given a new bed that's large enough to stretch out on. I can't find the words to express my glee and feel a lump form in my throat at the kind gesture. This cushion is far superior to the hard floor, yet I wonder how I'll transport it from room to room as Mom wanders around the house. I need one in every room.

Rachel eyes the bed warily, keeping her distance in case it's a threat. Dad pats the cushion beside me, inviting her to come closer. I lift my eyebrows and give her a reassuring head tilt. She shifts from paw to paw, takes a cautious step, then glances at Mom, who scratches behind her ears. My tentative sister leans into Mom and exhales a heavy sigh. Dad pats the bed again, and Rachel inches forward, checking in with Mom for approval. She circles the cushion, ensuring it's safe, and finally settles down beside it, resting her head on her paws.

Mom and Dad exchange a few words, and then Mom scoots over to crouch beside me on the bed. I lick the top of her other foot, feeling a sense of accomplishment. She rubs my back and reaches her other hand out to Rachel, who raises her eyebrows in response. Rachel struggles with change, and while I would gladly make room for her, I'm content to stretch out and claim this nap spot for myself.

Mom steps aside, and Dad lifts Rachel into his strong arms, placing her gently beside me. She hesitates for a moment, unsure of what to do. Then she warily sniffs the squishy cushion before hopping down to lie on the hardwood floor. Clearly, she doesn't trust it yet. Mom strokes her head reassuringly, and I hope she'll overcome her hesitation. The bed is delightful, and I wouldn't want Rachel to miss out on such a cozy spot. This is my new favorite place to lounge.

A few weeks later, I discover that the cushion has many useful functions. Mom and Dad are away on vacation and have entrusted our care to the kind couple that lives upstairs. Rachel and I have taken up residence in their apartment, and I've been loving every minute of our visit, although I do miss Mom and Dad. They're never gone for long because they miss me too much to stay away.

The couple lavishes attention on us, and I make an effort to lick their hands, legs, and faces to express my appreciation. The woman takes Rachel and me for a lovely afternoon stroll, encouraging us to enjoy the sunny day and bask in the warm sunlight before circling back to our building. I treasure my time with her, and I can tell that she loves animals.

I lope back into her apartment and make a beeline for my water bowl, slurping down mouthfuls of the cool liquid and quenching my thirst after the trot around the block. The heat makes me pant, and nothing soothes my parched tongue like a tall drink. A few drops dribble from my mouth and fall to the floor. I lick my lips and amble over to the comfortable bed, which the couple conveniently relocated to their living room. I appreciate the thoughtful gesture.

I curl into a ball and am about to drift off into an afternoon nap when I notice the couple packing up our bowls and bag of food. The woman holds out the leashes, and Rachel hops up enthusiastically, ready for another outing. I raise my eyebrows, roll onto my side, and close my eyes to express my disinterest. I'd prefer to rest for now and go for a walk later this evening, but the woman moves closer and dangles the leash in front of my nose. I look up at her, blinking in confusion. We went outside only moments ago, and I'm not inclined to get up. She doesn't understand and continues to murmur my name and stroke my neck. Then she gets to her feet and pats her thighs, saying my name a few times and beckoning me, but again, I decline to engage.

Rachel waits patiently, a broad grin on her face as she anticipates another walk. The woman confers with the man for a moment, glancing down at me lying on my bed, and my tail swings from side to side in anticipation. The woman leads Rachel toward the front door, and the man stoops beside me and grabs two corners of my bed. I look at him expectantly, wondering what he has planned. He lifts the corners and begins to walk backward, dragging the bed and myself along with it. He glances over his shoulder as he maneuvers it down the hallway and out the front door. I sit up and survey the situation, taking in Rachel's puzzled expression as she follows us.

The man pulls the bed to the elevator and pauses as we wait for the doors to emit the familiar ding and whoosh open.

Then he places the bed into the small compartment, and the four of us make the quick trip down several floors.

This fluffy cushion isn't just a comfortable spot to lounge—it becomes my regal chariot, carrying me effortlessly from place to place. I never realized it could serve this purpose, and the novelty makes me feel incredibly special. I'd happily take a daily ride straight to the building's front door, leaving plenty of energy for the neighborhood patrol.

When the doors open, Rachel leads the woman out of the elevator, and the man and I follow. I sit up and hold my head high, enjoying the attention and feeling like the queen of the building. My admirers are carting me about with such care and reverence, and I can't recall the last time that I felt so adored. I see the door to my apartment and begin to pant happily, thinking of home.

The woman opens the door, and the man grunts as he slides my bed across the threshold, down the hall, and into the living room. He pauses, breathing heavily, and pats me on the head. I give him an affectionate look as a thank you for his efforts. Rachel approaches and sniffs me, clearly baffled by this process. The couple waves goodbye and leaves us to rest after all the excitement.

I bury my head in the soft fabric and sigh contentedly. Just as I'm about to drift off into my long-overdue nap, I hear the front door open. Mom's voice drifts down the hall, and I immediately roll to my stomach, scrambling to my paws as Dad's heavy footsteps echo through the apartment. Rachel and I race forward to greet them at the door. Hugs and slobbery kisses fly in every direction. I press my face against

Dad's leg, nuzzling and leaving my scent and making it clear to everyone that he's mine.

Rachel whips her tail from side to side with reckless disregard for her surroundings, smacking the wall and then Mom's shin. I'm thrilled at their homecoming and want to show how much I missed them.

"Come see my chariot!" I cry excitedly. "You'll have to pull it, but it's amazing!"

I lead Dad into the living room and collapse onto my bed, waiting for the ride to begin. We will have such fun patrolling the halls, and I may even allow Rachel to take a turn.

*Rachel*

## Family Huddle

I dislike when Dad leaves the apartment each morning and doesn't return until the sun is setting. I wish that he would stay home and snuggle with me all day, taking breaks only for food and walks. I dream about a time when we can spend every moment together, watching TV, making lunch, exercising, and playing games. I'm used to our routine, but dogs have dreams too, and I spend my days figuring out how to achieve them. I've spent many afternoons sprawled out on the floor, wondering how to lock the door so Dad can't leave, although that would be problematic for my daily walks.

Then, something unexpected happened. It felt as though my wish had been granted because Dad decided to stay by my side day and night. I'm not sure who grants wishes, but I'm grateful for this one.

I expected Dad to depart at the appointed time, but instead of getting dressed and hurrying out the door, he rolled out of bed and took a seat in front of his computer, tapping away for hours on end. He now seems concerned and is concentrating on important tasks that I don't understand.

However, I'm elated that he's completing these duties from home, instead of disappearing to an undisclosed location.

He also reorganized his room, moving in a desk with a large screen and sliding the heavy dresser into the living room. I watched him curiously as he dragged the furniture around and tweaked the desk's position several times until he was satisfied. It's a special desk that can lift up and down with a whirring sound at the push of a button. Sometimes Dad sits in front of the screen, and sometimes he stands, shifting from foot to foot as he toils away. I'm so proud of him and never realized how hard he works. Now I just need to convince him to take afternoon naps with me. I'll keep wishing for that dream to come true.

As I sit by the bedroom doorway and contemplate the invisible line on the floor that still troubles me, I watch Dad tap his foot rapidly. He's murmuring to himself and periodically paces around the room, seemingly deep in thought. I tilt my head to one side and then to the other, wondering what complex ideas he's mulling over. Dad is very intelligent, and I'm confident that he can solve whatever riddle has stumped him.

Mustering my courage, I inch through the doorway, taking slow breaths to steady myself before entering another part of the house. Once safely in the bedroom, my excitement returns, and I wag my tail as I stroll up to Dad. I settle down beside his chair and gaze at him, which always lifts my spirits. Panting with delight, I savor these long days together. He scratches behind my ears while keeping an eye on the glowing computer screen. I notice black markings on a white background and wonder what the coded message could mean. Maybe it's part of a top-secret project and conceals sensitive information. That must be it! Wow! Now I'm even more impressed with Dad.

I take my responsibilities as the supportive canine seriously, knowing the security of our nation could be at stake. The risk makes me nervous, and I wonder if I'm up to the task. What if I accidentally discover a heavily guarded state secret? Could I sleep knowing I hold such critical information that can't be shared with anyone, not even Sara? I swallow hard, worried about how to handle such a complicated situation. Sara and I share everything, but if it's necessary for the good of the nation, then I'll keep Dad's secret. I raise my head and stick out my chest, ready to serve my country. Pride wells up within me, and I'm surprised at my willingness to tackle such challenging situations. Rachel, top-secret canine, reporting for duty, sir!

Dad pauses his tapping, turns to me, and uses both of his hands to scratch behind my ears. My concerns about the secret project fade away, and I lean my head against the side of his leg, basking in the attention. Who needs coded messages when they can enjoy head scratches and beg for back rubs? I guess it doesn't matter why Dad relocated his covert office to our home—I'm just glad to be involved. Who knows, we might be changing the world today.

Dad resumes his work, and I paw at his foot, letting him know that I would like more pets. He doesn't immediately respond, so I repeat the motion several times until he lovingly pats me on the head. I wag my tail excitedly and turn in a circle to show how much I appreciate the gesture. He murmurs my name but continues staring at the screen.

I settle down and take a moment to consider the situation. Clearly, he's doing something of great importance, so I ask myself, "What would a good dog do?" I sit obediently by his side, deciding that it's best not to bother him and instead, support him in his high-profile duties. I'll remain close by in case he requires my assistance, and I'll be ready to step in at a moment's notice.

I sit by his feet, and the morning passes quickly. I pace around the room with Dad when he gets up and then lie on the floor, wondering if I have the proper skillset to assist him when the time comes. At some point, I fall asleep, and when I awake, Dad is right where I left him. I'm relieved that I didn't miss anything during the unplanned nap. My eyes feel heavy, and I let myself drift back into a peaceful slumber, listening to the rhythmic clicking of the mysterious black keys.

The sound of food pinging in my metal bowl rouses me from my dreams. I spring to my feet and race over, ignoring the unsettling doorway, given food is at stake. Sara is a few steps ahead of me, and I hope that she doesn't inhale our lunch before I eat my fill. I slide to a halt in front of the bowls, nearly losing my footing on the slippery floor. I can't believe that I slept through Dad abandoning his post and serving our midday kibble.

I plunge my nose into the bowl, greedily gobbling up every morsel. The anxiety about learning state secrets has piqued my appetite. I must remain in top physical condition to handle any sensitive issues, so maintaining a healthy diet is essential. Lunch is an important part of my job, and I try to stay focused on inhaling my food, refusing to glance over at Sara for fear that I'll spill the beans. She doesn't appear interested in chatting because we're racing to make our lunch disappear. When my bowl is empty, I lick the bottom to ensure that no crumbs are left behind.

Dad takes us for an afternoon walk, which is delightful because he's usually working at this time of day. Midday walks with Dad are a special treat, and I savor the experience. When we return, I trot to the water bowl, feeling suddenly parched, and slurp down mouthfuls of cool liquid. It's important to stay hydrated, and I want to be prepared for anything, given the critical situation at hand.

Dad returns to his desk and quickly eats his lunch. I admire his ability to multitask because when it's my lunchtime, I can't focus on anything else until the bowl is empty and the floor has been surveyed for any stray kibble that flew out during my meal. I take up my former position by his side, boldly crossing through the doorway and refusing to let it break my stride. "Operation Get Things Done" is officially underway.

We spend the rest of the day together, and I help Dad complete tasks, staying close and alert. I cheer him on with periodic tail wagging and head nudges, letting him know that I notice his effort.

"You're doing an amazing job!" I say. "Keep up the exceptional work!"

I give Dad my full attention, and if I had a treat, I would offer it to him. Unfortunately, treats are in short supply, so I shake my head and focus on the task at hand. Top secret work demands concentration. We must complete the assignment to protect the safety and security of our fearless nation.

Suddenly, Dad starts talking to his screen, and I leap to my feet in surprise. I don't think the machine is alive, so why would he speak to it? I'm stunned to find that several small faces have appeared in boxes on the screen. I don't understand this behavior and stand there in shock with my mouth hanging open. The screen replies to Dad in different voices, and I watch the little people closely. Dad chats with them while I assess the situation, sniffing the air to determine if they smell like real people. I don't detect any new scents, and I'm confused about who these talking heads are. I've seen people on TV before, but Dad never holds a conversation with them. I rest my chin on the desk and lean toward the little people. Suddenly, I hear laughter, and Dad turns and affectionately rubs the top of my head.

My tail wags as Dad's attention settles on me. I pant softly and watch the tiny figures on the screen. Dad ignores them, so I treat them as harmless. I sit on my bum and study the interactions, eyes scanning each small box for any sign of a dog.

Over the next few days, we establish a routine, and I accept that the screen people are part of Dad's normal work activities; however, I remain alert and skeptical when they're around. You can never be too careful when strangers are in your house.

Mom visits on the days when Dad doesn't sit at the desk, and we spend time together doing indoor activities, which is fine by me. Maybe they've lost interest in the outside world and realize that all they need in life are Sara and me. We still go on three walks a day, so I'm pleased with our new arrangement. I've never received so many pets before, and the constant attention and companionship are a dream come true. If Mom moved in permanently, then everything would be perfect.

Leslie Popp

*Rachel*

## His Majesty

Dad is organizing the apartment and moving furniture around, which confuses me because our home was perfect the way it was. I don't mind a bit of redecorating and am willing to assist, but I fear that my paws are not equipped for this task. I can lean against objects to push them across the floor—at least I think I can. I haven't tried it, but I would be willing to experiment.

Dad has the situation under control and hasn't shared his plans with me, so I remain close by and monitor the proceedings. I eventually drift off to sleep with my cheek pressed against the cool floor, enjoying the feel of this toasty summer day. Sara lies close enough for my tail to reach her, and that comfort lets me slowly drift off after settling my racing mind. In my dreams, I walk along sunlit paths, chasing the pigeons I still hope to catch. Sure, they can fly, but they can't outrun me, and I would win a fight. Still, they stare with those beady eyes, like they know something I don't. To be fair, I've tried to catch one countless times, but

# The Bark Diaries

I always come home empty-handed. Clearly, I need a new strategy because my usual approach isn't working.

I awake to the sound of the front door opening and try to remember my dream. I had a genius plan to capture the flock of pigeons, but now the details have vanished. I concentrate, trying to commit the strategy to memory, but it's too late because the dream has disappeared into the recesses of my mind. I'll need to refocus on pigeons before my next nap and hope the plan resurfaces. It might require several naps, but I'm determined to recover my well-laid plot.

Mom enters the room, and I forget about the pigeons. Who can worry about silly birds when she's around? Mom is gingerly carrying a container with holes in the sides and a handle on top, and I wonder what precious cargo it hides. The front has a metal gate, and a pair of yellow eyes stares at me from the dark depths. My ears perk up in alarm and my eyes widen.

It's Pumpkin—the cat! I can't believe he's in our house.

"Did you see that?" I ask Sara, who pants contentedly. Then Mom disappears into the bedroom. I stare at the cat, heart racing. My ears stand tall, and my tail twitches. What does he want? What should we do?

My heart thumps as my mind races. I thought our night at Mom's apartment was a one-time deal. I never expected Pumpkin to visit our humble abode. How long will he stay? Where will he sleep? What will he eat? I just hope he doesn't touch my kibble. There's no way I'll let that happen.

Dad hauls Pumpkin's belongings into the apartment, and I watch the growing pile, my ears twitching and tail flicking with interest. There's a carpeted tower with a gently curved platform on top, a covered box filled with pebbles—or maybe sand—a stack of cans, a bag of food, a box of toys, and two bowls. I let out a quiet, contented huff at the sight of the cans and bowls, grateful that Pumpkin's meals are already sorted. Maybe he'll let me sample a taste of his cuisine.

"Do you think he'll share his food?" I wonder, glancing at Sara, who remains quiet but looks skeptical. "You're right, it's probably too soon."

Dad scurries around, organizing the cat's possessions and setting his food bowls on the table. Why is he allowed to eat at the table? I would also like a chair and to be given a plate if we're rethinking the seating chart. Sara and I promise not to lick anyone else's dish unless they need help finishing the leftovers. I'll happily step in to ensure nothing goes to waste.

I wait anxiously, unsure how to react to this novel situation. I've never expected a cat to show up here, and I feel completely unprepared. I wish I had a strategy for handling feline visitors.

The door to the bedroom opens, and Pumpkin wanders out, looking immaculately groomed with his orange fur, elegant stripes, and long whiskers. He walks on silent paws, taking purposeful steps and surveying the room. I look around, wondering what he thinks of our home. We lock eyes, and I squirm under his gaze, hoping that he won't approach me. I'm still recovering from the shock of seeing him again, and I'm not ready to engage. However, Sara seems thrilled to greet him and wags her tail as he strolls by.

Pumpkin assesses her before moving along to inspect the kitchen. Mom trails close behind, ready to assist him at a moment's notice.

Pumpkin holds his tail high, and it swishes with each step. I wish I were that graceful. My collar jingles when I walk, and my nails click against the wood floor, so you know I'm coming long before I'm sitting eagerly at your feet. Pumpkin trots about unnoticed, making himself known only when it's advantageous, which is concerning because he could easily sneak up on me. I try to calm my thundering heart and begin to pant heavily. My mouth feels dry, but I hold perfectly still, trying to avoid the cat's attention. He sniffs the perimeter of the kitchen and slips out of view, which heightens my anxiety. What is he doing? What is he looking for? What is he thinking?

Pumpkin reappears on the kitchen counter, surveying the room from his elevated perch, and takes a seat at the corner with his feet turned out and his tail hanging over the edge. He seems proud and sure of himself, and there's something regal and commanding about his presence. It instills fear in me, and I want to remain in his good graces. He looks at me, and I quickly drop my gaze to the floor, studying the wood grain. When I glance up, he's still watching me. I take a deep breath and hold his stare, keeping my head down to show that I'm not a threat. Mom gently strokes Pumpkin's head, and he closes his eyes and emits a soft rumbling noise that's filled with contentment.

Pumpkin spies his food dish on the table and hurries over to investigate. He takes a cautious bite, chews daintily, and seems satisfied. Next, he inspects the box of sand before wandering over to peer into my food bowl. I shift nervously, worried he'll snatch the crumbs I'd saved from lunch, but he only takes a long sniff, shakes his head, and walks away. Crisis averted!

Dad maneuvers the carpeted tower into the bedroom, and Pumpkin trots after him, clearly attached to this piece of furniture. Once Dad positions the perch by the window, Pumpkin rakes his claws down its side. Those long claws concern me, and I glance down at my blunt nails, worried that they'll be insufficient in a physical altercation.

"What should we do? Do you think he'll sleep on the couch with us?" I ask, glancing over at Sara. "Will he come on our walks, too?"

I have many questions, but only time will tell. Dad sits on the floor between Sara and me, and I lean against his leg, feeling reassured by his presence. He gently rubs our backs and speaks softly, saying Pumpkin's name a few times.

The cat appears in the bedroom doorway, tilting his head as he surveys us. Mom kneels beside us and encourages Pumpkin to approach. His gaze drifts from her to me and then back again, evidently skeptical about approaching. Then he sashays over with his head held high and his face expressionless. If it weren't for his wide eyes, I would think that he was completely unfazed by this sudden change of circumstances. I drop my head to the floor between my paws and watch him, feeling uncertain and scared. Dad continues to pet me as Pumpkin steps forward. He stops a few feet away and sniffs the air before circling and assessing me from all angles. He hops onto the coffee table, and I glance over my shoulder to see him staring down at me with an air of authority.

"Can I be of assistance, sir—?" I ask, wondering how I should address him. Should I call him Pumpkin, or Cat, or Mr. Cat, or Your Highness? He looks at me quizzically. "I'm sorry. I meant, Your Majesty."

It's difficult to read his reaction, but he doesn't appear displeased, so I assume "Your Majesty" is the correct title. I can't believe we have a king in our midst. I wonder if our apartment is part of his kingdom—it must be. Why else would he be visiting?

After a few minutes, I begin to relax, and Pumpkin saunters back into the bedroom, apparently satisfied with our home. I look at Sara, who seems intrigued by our visitor, and then take stock of Pumpkin's belongings, scattered around the house. I wonder if tonight marks an overnight visit or if he is moving in permanently.

Our interactions become less tense over the next few days, and I conclude that he means no harm. He enjoys his personal space and can generally be found perched on a high ledge with a sweeping view of the room. He's very active for short periods of time between naps, hopping on and off the furniture and exploring every inch of the apartment. Pumpkin has free reign of the place and doesn't hesitate to cross thresholds. I envy his confidence and admire his commanding personality. He prowls our home, exploring as if he owns the place, and if he's king, then I suppose he does. I show him the respect he deserves, and I'm always friendly and obedient. While he doesn't say it, I can tell that he's interested in Sara and me. If nothing else, he's curious and occasionally wanders over to take a closer look at me. I remain quiet and subdued, not wanting to scare him or invite any unwanted aggression. Those piercing eyes are unsettling, and I've concluded that cowering is the best approach.

After a week, we've fallen into a comfortable rhythm, and while we don't directly interact, we're on friendly terms. I closely observe Pumpkin's activities, seeking to learn more about our new ruler and his peculiar habits. He conducts perimeter checks at night, and I feel safer knowing that he's patrolling our borders.

Pumpkin enjoys sprinting around and chasing a small mouse toy. I find this incredibly entertaining and marvel at his speed and agility as he tosses it into the air, sprints after it, and carries it proudly in his jaws. This game is way better than any show on TV.

The most confusing habit is his passion for pushing small objects off tables, dressers, and shelves. He bounds atop the furniture and paws at any nearby trinkets until they crash to the floor. Then he stares down at them with a satisfied expression on his face and a mischievous twinkle in his eye. I'm not sure why he targets these objects: a pen, Dad's wallet, a few coins, a piece of paper, and a bottle of cream that Mom rubs into her hands. I'm sure he has a reason for his actions, but I can't figure it out, and I'm too embarrassed to ask. I don't want Pumpkin to think that I'm unintelligent, so I pretend to know exactly what he's doing. He pauses midway through clearing off the dresser and looks over at me, as though checking to see if anyone is watching and trying to stop him, before resuming his mission.

# The Bark Diaries

We've adapted to each other and have learned to coexist harmoniously. Pumpkin even sleeps on the pillow that's reserved for Mom. While I know that I'm too big to share the bed with Mom and Dad, I'm envious of Pumpkin for snuggling with her all night long. His size is definitely an advantage.

The days are filled with joyful moments, and I've come to accept Pumpkin as our leader. He shows respect for Sara and me, and Sara clearly likes him. She wags her tail whenever he walks by, though he doesn't return the gesture. I don't think cats wag, but don't quote me on that. I have limited experience with felines, yet I'm determined to be a good dog and befriend Pumpkin. After all, there's more than enough room on the couch for all of us, and I'm willing to share.

Leslie Popp

*Sara*

**Mom's Assistant**

I love to assist Mom with her daily activities because helping family members is very rewarding. My soft paws are not suited for certain tasks; however, when such situations arise, I remain by Mom's side, providing quiet encouragement and unwavering support. We all need praise every now and then, and I excel at bringing a positive attitude and a friendly smile to even the most mundane situation. I'm a valuable member of any team and an essential colleague to both Mom and Dad, who work hard in front of bright screens all day.

This morning began much like any other, with the blaring sound of Mom's alarm announcing the arrival of a new day. She always rises with the sun and collapses into bed when darkness falls. Morning is our quiet time together when only Mom, Rachel, Pumpkin, and I are awake. Pumpkin usually wakes us before the alarm with his determined meows and relentless attacks on the wobbly lampshade beside the bed. I don't mind his early morning performances because it means Mom will soon be up and ready to join me for a refreshing walk.

Today, Pumpkin follows the shriek of the alarm clock with an inquisitive meow, and I hear Mom roll over in bed, murmuring softly. Pumpkin has the honor of sleeping beside her, which makes me jealous, but I'm also thrilled that Mom has a snuggle buddy at night. I'm content to lounge on the couch with my sister curled up beside me.

A few minutes later, Pumpkin leads Mom into the kitchen, and I lift my head to watch with interest. The cat meows anxiously, urging her to hurry with his breakfast. He can be very demanding, and I respect his leadership and judgment. I accept him as the four-legged ruler of this residence and try to follow his rules and regulations. Despite being the smallest member of the household, he dominates the room and asserts his authority at every turn.

Once His Majesty finishes his breakfast and settles on his climbing tower to gaze out the window, Mom turns her attention to Rachel and me. We wag excitedly as she approaches, enjoying her playful pats on our backs. She slips into her shoes and grabs our colorful leashes. Rachel and I scramble to our paws, stretch, and prance around while Mom loops the leashes around our necks. We can never stay still for this part of the routine, but Mom doesn't mind, and soon we're ready for our morning adventure.

After another delightful outing in the crisp dawn air, we return home and enjoy mouthwatering treats. The flavor lingers on my tongue as I watch Mom, hoping for a second helping. I follow her to the counter, keeping the snack bag in sight and counting the minutes until lunch. I'm never sure exactly when it will be served, but I can usually guess based on how long it's been since my morning treat and the way the sunlight falls across the floor.

After dressing and washing her face, Mom is ready to start her busy day. She settles at the small desk in the living room and opens the laptop resting beside a large screen. The device hums to life, and I hear a fan whirring inside. I wonder what secrets the contraption might be hiding. Mom spends hours tapping away on the black keys, occasionally pausing for professional-sounding phone calls. Dad follows a similar routine in another room, so I figure they must work for the same company.

I watch Mom closely, listening to the familiar clacking of the keyboard. The sound fills the room and reassures me that she's nearby. She stares intently at the screen, wringing her hands as she works and clearly deep in thought. I'm proud of her dedication and want to make her life easier and more enjoyable. I don't understand the details of her work, but I can tell it must be important.

I amble over, glancing from Mom's face to the screen and back to her hands as they tap the keys. I don't know how to help because my paws aren't made for pressing the squares, so I stand patiently by her side. She glances down and coos softly, and I wag my tail furiously in response. I am such a loyal dog.

I take a step closer, stretch my neck out, and slide my nose beneath the arm of the chair and onto her lap. She pauses, says my name, and pats me on the head. Encouraged by this positive reaction and hoping that it's helping with her work, I shove my head further onto her lap. It's an awkward position, but I don't mind; I could stand here for hours. Mom tousles my head with one hand and taps the keys, sliding the mouse with the other. She's very talented and is excellent at multitasking, which really benefits our productivity. I gaze up at her, angle my nose toward her face, and begin to pant heavily.

She plants a kiss on my nose, and I shiver with delight. She resumes her task, and I stand by her side, feeling like an essential part of this operation and being careful not to disturb her flow. My gaze fixes on her elbow, and I stretch forward to deliver a slobbery lick. Mom startles at the wet intrusion but quickly returns to her work. I admire her determination and concentration because I am easily distracted by sounds, smells, and movement. I often spend a full hour daydreaming about food, which is why she's in charge.

As the slobber mark on her elbow dries, I stick out my tongue and lick it again, determined to praise and reward her. Mom rubs my neck, and I wiggle my butt happily, smacking my tail against the desk leg. I try to climb onto her lap, but the chair arm blocks me, so I roll the chair a few inches to the side instead.

Mom shifts her keyboard so it's squarely in front of her, seemingly unfazed by the change. The tapping resumes, and I listen contentedly, curious about what she's doing. I bet it's a high-stakes task that only she could handle. Maybe she's overseeing the kibble supply chain, making sure every dog receives their monthly shipments. It sounds like an essential job; in fact, it's probably the most important one. Wow, she's incredible! If other dogs knew about her responsibilities, she would be a celebrity in the canine community. I'll have to spread the word so she earns the respect she deserves. Work like hers should be rewarded with praise and maybe even a treat.

I stare up at her kind face, noticing the serious expression as she focuses on the screen. I wish I knew what she's thinking. I'm sure she's a genius, and her thoughts must be scholarly—beauty and brains all in one!

Her phone rings, startling me. She speaks briefly before hanging up, sighing heavily. I wonder who would be calling at this early hour. Dad isn't awake yet, and I don't know anyone else who works for their organization.

I take another enthusiastic step forward, pushing her chair further from the center of the desk. She adjusts the keyboard again, effortlessly returning to her work. I love that we can spend these quiet mornings together. It feels like a special time with just the two of us girls making our way in the big world, and I'm glad I can participate in her work. I'm probably the best assistant she has ever had. Who else is as loving, supportive, and patient as I am? I lick her leg for good measure, then rest my chin on her thigh in contentment.

My eyelids begin to droop as the tapping sound lulls me to sleep. I blink several times, trying to stay alert in case Mom needs me. It's important for an assistant to be awake and ready to respond in at moment's notice. You never know when your boss might require help or advice.

Despite my best efforts, I begin to doze off, and my legs nearly buckle underneath me. I catch myself and stumble forward, pushing Mom's chair away from the desk. She calls my name, and I freeze, surveying the situation. The keyboard is out of reach, and Mom is staring down at me. I give her an innocent expression and lift my eyebrows, hoping she isn't upset at the disruption.

She massages my neck, gently slides out from under my chin, and climbs awkwardly to her feet. I lift my head from beneath the armrest and look up at her questioningly. I hope we're done for the day because I could really use a nap. All this standing and offering support is exhausting, and the couch looks incredibly inviting.

Mom pats my head and says my name with a smile, then slides her chair back and returns to her work. I'm tempted to poke my head through the armrest and reclaim my spot. I cast a quick glance toward her lap. Across the couch, Rachel lounges like royalty, paws tucked neatly beneath her while she watches me with lazy curiosity. Curling up beside her, I sink into a comfortable position, ears twitching for any hint that Mom might need me. Soon, my head rests on my paws, and I drift into a peaceful, midmorning nap.

Leslie Popp

*Rachel*

**Road Trip**

Mom and Dad have been packing our belongings into cardboard boxes and stacking them in neat rows. I find this process unnerving, but Pumpkin loves it and leaps onto the towering stacks to gaze down at Sara and me with curiosity. He enjoys the elevated vantage points and hops from one pile to another as if navigating an obstacle course. His sharp yellow eyes follow our every move, and there's no place to hide. The boxes form a complex maze, and Pumpkin's size and agility let him slip through the narrow tunnels.

The couch is thankfully box-free, and I'm relieved that my cushioned throne is still available. I feel secure while curled into a tight ball on my favorite cushion. Nothing bad can happen while I'm nestled there—at least, I don't think so. I've been watching the packing with trepidation and worrying about the fate of our belongings. Are they being thrown away? Is this our new living situation? I don't want to navigate between box towers for long and would much rather reclaim the floor space. I like to sprawl in the entryway so everyone pets me as they come and go. It's a tried-and-true method for earning the maximum number of belly rubs, and I've had to temporarily put it on hold.

Pumpkin is staring at me from atop the tallest tower, and I find his piercing eyes unsettling. I'm at least three times his size, but his confidence, stealth, and air of authority are intimidating, and I give him plenty of space. He tilts his head to one side and flicks his tail nonchalantly, and I can't help but wonder why he's so interested in me. I lie here quietly, hoping the apartment will soon return to its normal state so I can enjoy some peace.

"Do you need something, Your Majesty?" I ask, hoping that it'll be a simple request.

Pumpkin doesn't answer. He tilts his head, lifts a paw and starts licking his toes, completely absorbed in the task. I let out a relieved sigh because my paws are off the hook…for now. One paw done, then the other, Pumpkin glances up and catches me staring. I snap my gaze away, feeling like I've been caught doing something naughty. Staring only draws his attention, and I silently tell myself not to make that mistake again.

Luckily, Pumpkin grows bored of watching me fret over the changes to our home décor and leaps between the boxes, settling on a stack in the corner. He examines the top of the box and begins fiddling with the flaps, gently lifting one and letting it flop back down. He pauses, considers his next move, shifts onto the adjacent box, and raises the flap again. Repeating the motion several times with one paw and then the other, he is completely captivated by this important task.

He sticks his head into the box, scrutinizing the contents and taking inventory to ensure nothing is missing. I think we should catalogue each item in case we need to locate something critical among the sea of boxes. I especially want to know where my extra food is stored. Pumpkin slides a paw into the box and digs around, shifting the contents as he explores the depths. After a few minutes, he seems satisfied and carefully steps back, letting the flap settle into place.

He glances around and notices me watching again, so I quickly look down at my paws. Pumpkin saunters over to investigate another box and loses interest in me. I sigh and drop my head between my paws, hoping for a few minutes of shut-eye.

The next day, unfamiliar men carry our belongings out of the apartment. I grow distressed as they maneuver my couch through the front door, worrying whether I'll ever see my cozy cushion again. Mom and Dad direct the process while the men work quickly, leaving only a few boxes and scattered items behind. After clearing out the last of our belongings, I walk across the bare floor, sniffing the air to find familiar scents. I pace the living room, listening to my nails click against the bare floor and noticing how much bigger it feels without furniture.

Dad leads Sara and me outside, and Mom carries Pumpkin in his chariot, which resembles a box with a cozy bed inside and a metal gate barring the entrance. We're loaded into a car, and I gaze out the window as we rumble away. The vehicle is packed with the remaining boxes, Pumpkin's climbing tower, and bags of dog food. I'm relieved to see that we're well-supplied in case I have the urge to snack. The world rushes by, and the landscape eventually transitions to wide open spaces as we travel beyond the city limits. I enjoy watching the other cars zoom by and spot several dogs looking back at me. I'm so excited that we're going on an adventure!

We pass through unfamiliar cities and drive along roads lined with lush forests. Music blares from the speakers, and Mom and Dad sing along enthusiastically. The mood is infectious, and I study their smiling faces as they bounce to the rhythm. The words escape me, but the beat makes me wiggle and sway.

We detour off the main road and stop alongside a building displaying a brightly lit sign over the front door. As Mom rolls down the window, a delicious smell permeates the air and delights my nose. My ears tilt forward, and drool drips from my mouth. Peering into the front seat, I see Mom accept a paper bag from a man leaning out of a small window. The car lumbers forward and pauses again in the parking lot.

Mom and Dad dig through the bag and begin to chow down on the pungent food, glancing warily at Sara and me. Sara inches forward, stretches her neck into the front seat, and tries to snag a few crumbs. I would also like a taste but opt to wait patiently to see if any morsels are dropped on the ground. I usually get dibs on floor food. The scents of grease and salt perfume the confined space, and I try not to drool in anticipation.

Finally, Dad turns in his seat and holds out a golden twig that glistens with oil. I snatch the treat from his hand, and the salty flavor and crunchy texture dazzle my taste buds. Sara devours her treat, tail wagging in delight. I watch Dad intently, hoping for another bite, but he finishes the last one, sighs contentedly, and pats his stomach. I hope we make another stop soon because I could easily finish an entire box of those potato slivers. Next time, I'll have to claim a container of my own from the man in the window.

We continue our journey, and the sun is now high in the sky, beating down on the car and making it a bit too toasty for my liking. Eventually, we turn off the main road and into a parking lot filled with unfamiliar people and dogs. The area is wooded, and there's a lovely patch of grass where dogs are strolling around with their noses pressed to the ground. Dad unloads us from the car, and we join the ranks of pups patrolling the area, stopping to sniff a few butts, have a drink from our bowl, and gobble up some snacks, although I'm too anxious to eat much of the kibble. I don't encounter any of the neighborhood dogs, and the smells here are unfamiliar. Everyone we meet is friendly, but I'm uncomfortable around new dogs, preferring to keep to myself and remain by Dad's side. The world can be an intimidating place.

Our pit stop is brief, and after a few minutes in the fresh air, we return to the car and roll away, zipping along at a thrilling pace. The sun begins to sink, the sky grows dark, and the moon casts a silvery glow on the weary world. We've traveled a long distance, and I'm impatient to reach our destination. Pumpkin begins to meow, escalating from a soft, questioning noise to a pitiful, distressing sound, and I worry that something is terribly wrong. Mom is alarmed by his persistent yowling, and when we arrive at a large building constructed from heavy stone blocks, she leaps

## The Bark Diaries

from the vehicle, snatches up his carrier and our leashes, and hurries toward an unfamiliar door. To my surprise, she flings it open to reveal a cozy apartment.

I stand in the entryway, wondering if I'm allowed to be here. I don't know who owns this place, and I don't want to intrude. Pumpkin strolls out of his carrier and begins to explore, unconcerned with the question of ownership. Mom and Dad unload the car and stack our belongings in a disorganized pile in the middle of the room. Mom sets out food and water bowls, places Pumpkin's sandbox in the corner, and slides his climbing tower across the room to the large window. She and Dad sink onto the couch, exhausted from the long trip.

Pumpkin inspects his bowls, disappears into the sandbox, and emerges looking relieved. He patrols the perimeter of each room, making careful notes about the surroundings and scrutinizing every nook and cranny. He's an inquisitive cat and quickly lays claim to the residence. Leaping onto the kitchen table, he surveys the area, holding his head high and turning out his toes in an elegant pose. His profile is striking, and he is a born leader. I'm glad that Pumpkin is part of our family.

I stand frozen in the living room, feeling uncertain and trying to decide whether the space between the couch and the opposite wall constitutes a threshold. There are many smells, and my nose twitches as I catalog them. Recent occupants have left their scents on the couch. I take a few hesitant steps, sniff around the entryway, and note that another dog was here as well. The smell is old though, which suggests that he moved away months ago.

## Leslie Popp

Mom and Dad dig through the boxes and suitcases, removing fresh clothes and toothbrushes. I stand quietly in the hallway, watching them move from room to room. The cat lounges peacefully on the bed, stretching out after claiming the apartment and choosing a pillow.

This whole situation is confusing because I thought we were visiting relatives, but we're the only ones here. I gaze around and decide that I would be glad to call this apartment home if it pleases Mom and Dad. The couch looks cozy, the windows are large, and the floor is refreshingly cool. It'll take a few days to settle in, but I can adapt. I'll begin mapping out the neighborhood tomorrow on the morning walk, which is only a few hours away.

I lie on the floor, exhausted from the excitement of the trip. I consider hopping onto the couch, but Sara is already asleep on the ground, and I want to remain by her side. The room is homey, and the floor is acceptable for naps. I curl up with my back pressed against hers, and she wags her tail to show that she's happy to snuggle. Resting my head on my paws, I drift off into a deep sleep.

## *Rachel*

## Our New Happy Home

Golden sunlight streams across the room and wakes me up. Mom raises the blinds, prompting Pumpkin to leap onto his tower for a better look at the neighborhood. His tail hangs over the edge and sways in a slow rhythm while Mom gently strokes his head. He braces a paw on the windowsill, presses his nose to the glass, and surveys the neighborhood.

I blink myself awake, yawning as the final remnants of sleep cling to my eyes. I was too exhausted and nervous last night to fully evaluate this residence, but it feels far more welcoming in the morning light. Plump couch cushions promise excellent naps, and the open layout makes it easy to track Mom as she moves from room to room. Pictures of flowers brighten the walls, and I admire the natural décor—particularly the two suspiciously identical plants sitting on the kitchen and living room tables.

I scoot toward the greenery on the low table in front of the couch and study the vibrant stems. Nothing about the scent matches any plant that I've encountered on my walks, and each leaf is unnervingly symmetrical. My doubts are growing, and I'll need to consult Sara. This suspicious plant might be fake or an alien pretending to be a plant, and I intend to monitor it closely.

The pungent aroma of fish hits my nose, and I turn my gaze toward the kitchen, where Mom is shuffling around, and Pumpkin is meowing persistently. A moment later, she strolls into the living room and places a white dish on the table. Pumpkin leaps up beside it and begins to greedily chow down.

Mom kneels between Sara and me and scratches our backs while Sara enthusiastically licks her arm. I lie quietly, enjoying her attention while watching Pumpkin discreetly. If he drops any food on the floor, I'll hurry over to clean it up. Mom slides her feet into the shoes by the door and picks up our leashes. I jump to my feet and prance around excitedly. We're going for a walk! She lassos Sara and me and leads us into the warm morning sunshine.

There is lush grass underfoot, trees of all varieties dotting the yards and lining the sidewalks, and flowers blooming everywhere. The air smells clean, and the street is empty. I wonder where the yellow cars have gone, where the hordes of people are hiding, and why I don't detect the delightful aroma of cheesy pizza. Everyone must still be sleeping. As we wander down the street, I pause at every bush, light pole, and mailbox, sniffing carefully to catalog the scents of several neighborhood dogs I'll need to meet.

Quaint houses line the streets, with cars parked in driveways and colorful gardens decorating the yards. My ears twitch as I search for the sound of car horns honking, but the usual city noises are absent. Sunlight streams down, which feels unusual after living in the shadows of the tall city buildings for so many years. I lift my gaze, watching fluffy clouds drift lazily across the sky. The air is warm, and a gentle breeze ruffles my fur. I think I'm going to like it here.

We continue exploring, and I mark each street corner so the locals will know we've arrived. Birds chirp from the branches overhead, but I don't see any pigeons. These creatures are smaller and avoid the sidewalk, preferring to hop about in the treetops and monitor us from a safe distance.

My nose picks up an earthy scent, and I'm drawn to the acorns scattered around the next yard. Before Mom can react, I snatch one, chew quickly, and swallow my prize. Mom is immediately alarmed and crouches down to peer into my mouth, as though there's any evidence left of my snack. Mentally noting this house, I pant happily, already planning to lead Dad here on our afternoon walk. Sighing, Mom rises to her feet, and we continue along, inspecting every house on the street.

Sara is excited and keeps her nose close to the ground as she catalogs the many smells. She stands in a sunny spot, holding her head high, and letting the golden rays beat down on her.

We roam the neighborhood, sniffing for any sign of tasty restaurants. Not a single bagel bite appears, leaving me disappointed and concerned. I dive into a flower bed, inhaling the rich scent of soil and pollen. My eyes squeeze shut, and I sneeze violently, shaking my whole body and sending petals twirling into the air. I watch them float for a moment before settling onto the grass.

## Leslie Popp

Mom gently tugs on my leash, and I proceed to the next house. A little girl and her mom wander down the driveway, and I wag my tail to greet them. The girl points at me gleefully and jumps up and down.

"Dogs!" she calls with a warm smile on her face. "Look at the doggies!"

"Hi! It's very nice to meet you!" I exclaim, tilting my ears and lifting my eyebrows in a welcoming expression.

She pulls her mom toward us, and I step forward, lowering my head so she can scratch my back. I wag my tail, wiggle with delight, and let my mouth fall open as she rubs my fur. Sara leans in and plants a wet kiss on the girl's face, making her giggle. The sound is sweet, and the little girl admires our soft fur and floppy ears, lifting one of mine and letting it fall back down.

I sniff her hand, catching a faint scent of something sweet—maybe she ate a donut for breakfast. I consider licking her fingers but restrain myself; after all, we've only just met. Then my nose detects a delightful aroma wafting from her pink lunchbox. The scents of fresh bread, cheese, meat, and a hint of tangy sauce tease my senses, and my mouth waters at the thought of a meaty sandwich. That's not my food, and I would never snatch it from my new friend. I'm being such a good dog, meeting nice people on my very first day in the neighborhood. I bet there are more little kids around here eager to pet me and examine my floppy ears. The mother guides the girl toward the car, and I hope we cross paths again soon.

We make slow progress, my nose directing me along a meandering path—there's just so much to take in. Mapping your territory is important, and I'm overwhelmed by the novel sights, sounds, and scents. I pause beside a particularly pungent trash can at the end of an empty driveway, and the familiar aroma of pizza drifts from its depths. Tugging on my leash, I strain against Mom's hold, eager for a closer sniff and secretly hoping an unattended slice lies nearby. I would gladly make such a greasy treat disappear, but Mom pulls me back and steers us away from the house. Begrudgingly, I follow her, glancing over my shoulder and vowing to try again on the next walk. I mark this house as well, adding it to my list of favorites. Any place that smells like pizza is alright by me.

 A flash of movement catches my eye, and I swivel my head, suddenly on high alert. Something scurries around the base of a nearby tree, and I spot the tip of a bushy tail hovering a foot off the ground. I lead Mom toward the suspicious critter, my eyes fixed on the target. The tail twitches, and I quicken my pace, desperate for a better look at this local wildlife. Circling the tree, I finally see that the tail belongs to a small, furry body with oversized ears. Its tiny paws cling to the rough bark, allowing it to scale the vertical surface with ease.

 I pause, tilting my head to one side and then the other as I watch the creature. I've encountered squirrels before—they're nearly as fascinating as pigeons—but they were rare in the city. I'm glad that one has decided to make our neighborhood its home.

 The squirrel spots us, which is not surprising since I wouldn't describe Mom and Sara as stealthy. Each step they take crunches loudly on the leaves and acorns peppering the sidewalk, giving us away. The squirrel freezes, and I lunge forward, dragging Mom along. She calls my name, but there's no time to waste. If we don't act quickly, this swift rodent will scale the towering oak and escape. I'm quick, but Mom's grip on my leash slows me down, and the squirrel springs into action. With remarkable agility, it scampers up the trunk, flicking its tail wildly.

"Drat!" I cry, pausing at the base of the tree and craning my neck to assess the situation.

The squirrel perches on a high branch, peering down at us with a skeptical expression. I lock eyes with it, silently hoping it might topple from its perch and land in my waiting paws. I love a thrilling chase, and this nimble critter is a worthy opponent. Unfortunately, it remains securely seated on the branch, teasing me with its stillness.

Mom tugs on my leash, but I plant my paws firmly, unwilling to abandon the hunt. The squirrel seems perfectly at ease in its lofty perch, showing no sign of descending while I'm nearby. With the chase paused, I trot after Mom, scanning for other crafty critters that might want to play. I relish a competitive game of pursuit!

We turn at the next corner, and our home comes into view. My tail flicks with excitement as I wonder if Dad is awake yet. He's not a morning person and always silences the screeching alarm multiple times before finally rolling out of bed. That's why Mom joins us for the morning walk, and Dad is responsible for the afternoon stroll.

I stop abruptly, spotting an unusual animal slithering into a bush. Its body is skinny, its skin scaly, and its tail whip-like. I've never seen anything like it, and I wonder whether it poses any danger. It measures only a few inches, and I could easily crush it beneath my paws, but it's always wise to exercise caution when dealing with wildlife. I give the bush a wide berth, and glance over my shoulder to ensure nothing follows us. Movement ahead on the sidewalk catches my attention, and I notice another of these animals stretched across the path, soaking up the morning sunlight.

Mom doesn't break her stride and continues toward the creature. I follow at her heels, feeling uncertain and wondering if we should walk in the street instead. As we approach, the lanky critter scampers through the grass and vanishes into the flower bed. I scan the area, waiting for it to reappear. Mom pats my head and says something that sounds like "lizard." I don't recognize this word, but it seems menacing. I'll have to study these lizards closely and learn their habits to assess their threat level.

We enter the house, and I trot to my water bowl, lapping up the cool liquid and spilling a few drops on the floor. Sara flops down in the middle of the room, panting from the exertion. What a successful outing! This place is amazing, and I can't wait for our afternoon patrol.

Leslie Popp

*Sara*

# My Friend Pumpkin

I'm proud to be one of Pumpkin's closest friends. His orange fur is soft, his vibrant stripes look regal, and his piercing yellow eyes scrutinize everything around him—including me. Pumpkin is a cat of few words, but his tail, posture, and unblinking stare leave no doubt about what he's thinking. After he settled into the apartment, he organized the household and naturally assumed a leadership position. He's confident and fair, and even though I'm still learning his expectations, I'm happy to follow his guidance. The rules are new and confusing right now, but soon they'll feel natural.

I try to accommodate Pumpkin's preferences and respect his decisions and regulations. I've always been good at following instructions. For example, I know that peeing in the house is unacceptable, human food on plates is not meant for my lunch unless it's specifically offered to me, and exposed knees and elbows are prime for licking. We must all live by a code, and mine is simple: obey rules, be adorable, and love my humans.

# The Bark Diaries

Pumpkin is a complicated individual who has introduced new ideas and concepts into our lives. He assigned the comfy couch in the living room to Rachel and me, although Mom's desk remains off-limits. I don't mind this division of space because the couch is my preferred nap spot. Staying near the door lets me monitor the comings and goings of my family and greet Mom and Dad when they return. I'm always ready to hop up and wag enthusiastically to show my delight at seeing their familiar faces. How else would they know how much I missed them?

Pumpkin's domain encompasses the rest of the house, which seems disproportionate to his size. Rachel and I are much larger, and I assume that entitles us to more space. I didn't make up the rules and can't grasp Pumpkin's reasoning. Thinking about managing household matters makes my head spin, so I focus on what I enjoy most: licking hands and soaking up every ounce of affection. I'll let the others handle the serious decisions.

I enjoy watching Pumpkin patrol the house, ensuring we're safe and secure. I admire his diligence as he perches on his carpeted tower and stares out the window with unwavering focus. From this strategic vantage point, his keen eyes scan the neighborhood, noting the presence of any suspicious activity or characters. He is an excellent sentry, and I'm certain anyone seeking to harm us would cower under his intense glare. Pumpkin carries himself with authority and a no-nonsense attitude, so I wouldn't dare cross him and risk ending up on the wrong side of his sharp claws and gleaming teeth.

I'd love to give him a thorough sniff, but he insists on keeping his distance, which I've mostly learned to respect. Still, my curiosity and friendly nature draw me in, and I can't resist sneaking a closer look.

This morning, Pumpkin was perched on the corner of Mom's desk, eyes fixed on Rachel and me as we lounged on the floor. I held his gaze, wondering what thoughts might be swirling in his clever mind. He looked serious and deliberate, studying us closely, and I could only guess the important ideas he was analyzing.

I rose to my paws, hesitating for a moment as I considered the situation, wondering if I was making the right move. Slowly, I approached his perch, keeping my eyes on him and plastering an inviting smile across my face as I panted. He shifted his weight from paw to paw, his tail flicking in a steady rhythm. I froze, unsure what those subtle movements meant. Pumpkin continued to watch me, so I took another step forward and wagged my tail in a welcoming manner. He tilted his head, tracking my every move with those sharp yellow eyes. I swallowed nervously and glanced over my shoulder at Rachel, who was following my progression with keen interest.

I stretched my neck forward and sniffed the air around Pumpkin's paws. We still had a safe nose-length distance between us, but he immediately leaned back. Acting on instinct, I took another step closer and sniffed his toes.

In an instant, a furry paw landed a firm whack on the bridge of my nose. It didn't hurt, but I jerked back in shock. I blinked and glanced around with wide eyes, trying to understand what had just happened.

Pumpkin stared at me, already composed after the rebuff, and I shook my head, trying to untangle my swirling thoughts. Maybe I'd moved too quickly and crowded him, leaving him no choice but to push me away. Clearly, I'd need to try a different approach.

On my next attempt, I slowly shuffled forward, looking around nonchalantly. The position seemed non-threatening, and I dipped my head as I drew near, pausing to inspect the floor and sniff the leg of the desk. Pumpkin watched me closely, evaluating each step. I'd hoped he'd understand that I wasn't trying to claim his perch; I merely wanted his permission to sniff his paws, tail, and nose, if allowed.

I raised my head and took a deep breath, inhaling his unique scent and trying not to invade his space. He smelled of the clay in his sandbox, the fish he ate for lunch, and like Mom, whom he always sleeps beside and lovingly rubs against. Mom's familiar scent pleased me, and I took another long sniff.

Pumpkin shifted uncomfortably but didn't run away or swat my nose. I risked an innocent glance into his eyes and raised my eyebrows, a gesture that usually gets a favorable response from humans. Pumpkin remained still, holding my gaze. I averted my eyes again, not wanting to make him uneasy, and I considered my next move.

I took a hesitant step, dropped my head in submission, and then slowly lifted it until it was level with Pumpkin's primly turned-out paws. His tail was draped over the edge of the desk, and the end twitched as I drew near. I paused and waited for him to react. When nothing happened, I continued to raise my head.

Pumpkin moved with such speed that I barely registered his action until it was too late. This time, he didn't swat me but placed one paw atop my nose, pressed down, and angled my face toward the floor. We stayed like that for several seconds before I shook him off and stepped back. That was certainly progress because he was now providing guidance instead of bopping me on the snout. If he doesn't want me staring, I can work with that. I'm perfectly happy to stand near him and sniff his toes while looking away. It's not a difficult task.

Feeling pleased with myself, I loped over to Rachel and curled up by her side. She glanced from me to Pumpkin and back again, and I sniffed her face and ears. She returned the gesture, and I felt proud. Pumpkin's eyes remained fixed on us, watching the friendly greeting I had offered. Maybe next time he'd be open to a companionable sniff. I promised myself I'd try again tomorrow.

Pumpkin has many intriguing toys, and I love watching him chase them around the house, toss them high into the air, and let them crash to the floor. He slides them across the hardwood, dashes after their fleeing forms, and tackles them with expert precision. They lie quietly at his feet and concede defeat, which always impresses me.

I've considered joining in the romp, but I've never been fond of toys or playtime, so I monitor the situation from a safe distance. I wouldn't want the mouse toys to come after me in my sleep. For my peace of mind, I prefer to leave them alone and let Pumpkin handle the mice.

Tonight, he stalks his favorite mouse with purple fur and black eyes, while I stretch out on the floor, careful to remain quiet so as not to disturb the hunt. Pumpkin circles his prey, crouching low and padding silently across the room. He is a formidable hunter, moving gracefully as he assesses his target. His stealth is unsettling, and he could sneak up behind me if I weren't paying attention. In contrast, the jingle of my collar and the click of my nails on the hardwood announce my every move. I wish I had Pumpkin's skills.

He pauses, eyes locked on the unsuspecting mouse, and I hold my breath. The mouse hasn't noticed him, and the room practically vibrates with tension. I stay perfectly still, my gaze alternating from Pumpkin to the mouse and back again. That little mouse has no idea what's coming!

With a burst of speed and energy, Pumpkin springs forward, pinning the mouse beneath his mighty paws. His claws dig into the toy's soft fur, a clear display of his training and arsenal of homemade weapons. Pumpkin grabs the purple rodent by the tail and flings it high into the air. It arcs across the room, landing with a thud and rolling several times before coming to a stop. Pumpkin pounces again before it can regain its wits, swatting it solidly as it slides across the slick floor, careening toward me with alarming speed.

The toy halts just a few inches from my paws, and I eye it warily. My heart pounds as I anticipate its next move. I want no part in this skirmish and prefer to remain a passive spectator. Pumpkin saunters over, and our eyes meet. I glance back at the toy, concerned that it could strike at any moment. Pumpkin stalks the mouse, and a growing unease grips me. I don't like the look in his eyes and worry that his predatory focus might shift toward me. I turn and scramble away, putting as much distance as possible between myself and Pumpkin's arena.

I flop down in the center of the living room, satisfied that the tussle with the toy will not reach me here. Pumpkin has claimed most of the house for his games, and he rarely ventures into this room, making it a safe haven. I rest my head on my paws and let out a deep, contented sigh.

Pumpkin stares at me with a curious expression, his tail swaying gracefully. Then he turns back to the mouse, tossing it in the opposite direction and giving chase the moment it leaves his mouth. The scuffle continues for several minutes, and I marvel at Pumpkin's stamina, speed, and power. He is a true warrior and a fearless leader, and I feel privileged to be part of his inner circle.

Once the mouse threat has been neutralized, Pumpkin curls up in a sunny patch on the floor, lifting his head to enjoy the warm rays. Now that the excitement has passed, I close my eyes, reassured by the presence of such a skilled fighter nearby. I'm certain Pumpkin could handle any threat and protect us all.

## Rachel

### Beach Vibes

Grandma, Grandpa, and my uncle are visiting for a few days, and there's nothing I love more than a house full of friendly people who lavish me with back rubs. When one person is busy, I wander off to find another and sit patiently by their side until they bend down and scratch behind my ears. Laughter, hugs, and the inviting aroma of family meals shape what feels like the perfect life.

It's a beautiful sunny afternoon, and preparations are underway for an outing. Dad carries towels to the car at the curb, and I wonder how he'll use them. I enjoy road trips and am content to stare out the window as the world rushes by. Mom leads Sara and me to the car, and Dad hoists us into the back, carefully closing the door and ensuring our tails are securely inside. My heart thumps in my chest, and excitement bubbles up at the prospect of a family outing.

The car rumbles down the street, as I watch us make several turns, pick up speed, change lanes, turn again, and eventually enter a parking lot full of people and dogs. My ears perk up—why are there so many animals here? It seems unusual that everyone has a furry companion. The vehicle comes to a stop, and I leap to the ground as soon as the door opens. Dad fumbles for my leash before I wander too far away, then helps Sara down, since her disabled leg prevents her from jumping. She and I exchange quizzical glances, taking in the unfamiliar surroundings.

"There are so many dogs. Do you think it's the vet?" I ask suspiciously.

"I don't see any white coats, and I've never been to an outdoor vet," she responds, raising her eyebrows and shaking her head. "I don't think it's the vet."

Relief floods through me as I follow Dad toward a fenced-off area. The sound of crashing water fills my ears, and the scent of salt seeps into my nostrils. A gentle breeze ruffles my fur, and I lift my head, letting my mouth hang open as the sun warms my face.

Dad opens a gate with a loud squeak and guides us inside. Fine sand shifts beneath my paws and squishes between my toes as I take a few tentative steps. Lowering my nose, I sniff carefully, taking in the salty aroma and unsteady footing. Sara pauses beside me, sniffing eagerly and nudging me aside as she examines a broken shell. Glancing around, I follow Dad's gentle tug on our leashes as he leads us away from the closed gate.

My legs feel wobbly as my paws sink in the soft sand, and I struggle to maintain my balance. Sara moves slowly, and she appears skeptical of these unfamiliar surroundings when Dad removes our leashes. The lack of the familiar tether is unsettling because I enjoy staying physically connected to Mom or Dad, and without it, I worry they might wander off. I prefer to remain within a ten-foot radius of them at all times, but they clearly have other plans, encouraging me to explore independently.

I take a moment to assess the scene. A shaggy Golden Retriever, reminiscent of a young Sara, chases a tennis ball, kicking up clouds of sand. The game looks fun, but I'm content to watch. Another dog lounges between her owner's feet, shaded beneath a picnic table. A metal bowl brims with water nearby, and a toy rests between her front paws.

The sound of crashing water catches my attention, and I turn toward the towering waves racing up the gentle slope toward me. I shiver because this is the largest, most intimidating bathtub I've ever seen. The water is dark and threatening, and the noise unsettles me. Another wave hurls small shells and rocks onto the beach before dragging them back into the invisible depths. I'll be sure to steer clear of the churning water.

Suddenly, an orange ball sails through the air, and a black dog streaks past, heading straight for the waves. The ball lands in the surf and bobs up and down with the current. The dog plunges headfirst into the foaming water, sending spray flying as it frantically paddles toward the ball. My muscles tense, and my anxiety spikes as I watch this daring feat. I've never seen anything like it, and I fear for the brave dog's safety. In my opinion, that ball is lost and will never be retrieved, yet this dog refuses to admit defeat. It makes steady progress through the choppy water, keeping the ball in its sights as it is carried down the beach.

To my surprise, the dog captures the runaway ball between his teeth and turns toward the shore, paddling confidently while the waves propel him forward. He scrambles onto the sand, water streaming from his ebony fur. He appears to be proud of himself, and I admire his strength and determination. He shakes, sending sparkling droplets flying as his fur fans out in all directions. The dog strolls by, panting heavily, and drops the ball at his dad's feet. He sits patiently, eyes fixed on the colorful toy, until the dad hurls it again into the surf.

"Wait, what?" I exclaim, eyes wide as the black dog plunges back into the water. "He just rescued the ball from the waves, and the man threw it back? That can't be right."

The dog repeats the cycle several times, and I quickly decide it's a game I would rather not join. If it involves plunging into the waves, then count me out. Mom insists I'm a water dog, but I disagree. Water is best when it stays in my bowl and nowhere else.

I hear my name, and my head swivels toward the familiar sound. Dad and Grandpa are strolling down the beach and beckoning to me. I hurry toward them, eyeing the intimidating waves as they lap at the sand. Dad pauses at the edge of the surf, and I cautiously approach, feeling uncertain about the proximity to the natural bathtub. He is unconcerned with the noise and the prospect of getting wet, and I tell myself that everything will be okay. I stand by his side, watch the water as it rushes in and out, and try to remain composed.

Grandpa scratches behind my ears and pats my side, and I gleefully wiggle my butt. My mouth falls open, my tail begins to wag, and I temporarily forget about the risk of getting my paws wet. I look up at Grandpa's smiling face, trying to convey how much I appreciate his attention. I lean against his leg and encourage him to rub my back. Then a wave rushes toward us, shattering the beautiful moment and forcing me to retreat a few steps before it surges forward and touches my feet. We can't have that!

"No!" I bark, staring down the foaming water. "You do not touch my paws. Bad water! Bad waves!"

I hope that my firm tone will deter the water from attempting such an underhanded trick again. Soggy paws are the worst, and I don't want to smell like salt for the rest of the day. I stay a few feet behind Dad, who seems content to let the waves lap against his shins, exfoliate his feet with the rough sand, and coat his skin in salt. I'll maintain a safe distance and watch for any signs of distress. I don't want to leave Dad alone with the pesky waves, but I also don't want to engage, so I hope that it doesn't come to that.

I glance around, searching the beach for the rest of our party. Mom and Grandma are wandering around the other side of the fenced-in area and scanning for shells, which are attractive but not particularly impressive. Sara has positioned herself on the concrete slab near the entry gate, having decided that she doesn't like the feel of sand between her toes. She can be very particular, and after a short perusal of the area, she is ready to go home. I don't blame her, given the water is unnerving and the shifting sand is concerning.

The sun beats down on my fur, and I pant heavily to cool off. Near Sara, a green hose lies coiled, recently used by people to rinse their feet and give their dogs a drink. I lick my lips, imagining that refreshing liquid on my tongue.

Mom kneels beside Sara, rubbing her neck, and murmuring enthusiastically. She gives her a gentle hug, and Sara responds with a wet kiss on Mom's cheek. I dash over, eager for a hug, and Mom gladly obliges. I pant happily in Mom's ear because hugs are the best!

The sound of the hose draws my gaze, and Mom turns to see what has captured my attention. A hint of understanding flashes across her eyes, and she makes a beeline for the running water. I trail close behind, waiting anxiously as another dog takes a long drink. The hose is passed to Mom, and she calls me over, pointing at the stream of water and the enticing puddle it has formed. Slowly, I lower my head, sniff the puddle, and begin lapping up the liquid. I'm skeptical about drinking straight from the hose, but I enjoy a good puddle. A few drops splatter onto my nose and soothe my hot skin. I drink ravenously until I'm full and can hear the liquid sloshing around in my belly. I lick the droplets off my nose and glance over at Sara, who seems content in her current position and uninterested in the hose.

The rest of the family approaches, and we gather around Sara, who flashes a goofy smile at everyone. Dad secures the leashes around our necks, and we exit through the metal gate. The ride home is quiet, and I'm blissfully exhausted from the excitement after so many new sights and smells. What a wonderful day!

Mom brushes the remaining sand from our paws before we enter the house, but I still leave a trail of fine grains behind as I pad across the hardwood floor. Pumpkin greets us in the living room, looks me over, and takes a long sniff before wandering over to Mom, begging for attention. She bends down and kisses him on the head. I feel guilty that he couldn't join us at the beach, but I don't think he would have enjoyed the water. Besides, he already has a sandbox in the house.

I hop onto the couch and turn in a circle three times before lying down and resting my head on my paws; a lingering whiff of salt greets my nose. Sara curls up beside me with a quiet sigh. From his perch on Mom's desk, Pumpkin studies us intently, tilting his head back and forth before finally flopping down and closing his eyes.

I'm lucky to have such a wonderful family that loves me unconditionally. I can't imagine life without them, and I hope we stay this way forever. I don't care where we live as long as Mom, Dad, Sara, and Pumpkin are with me.

Leslie Popp

*Pumpkin*

## Pumpkin Sets the Record Straight

Sara and Rachel have done a wonderful job documenting our adventures, and I was thrilled to let them take the lead on this book. Their hard work freed up more time to nap on the windowsill. Still, I need to set a few things straight.

First, when the dogs call the house "our home" or "my home," what they really mean is, "Pumpkin's home, which we are allowed to live in because he is a gracious and benevolent ruler." That point is probably obvious, but I want to make it clear. Don't get me wrong, I love my mom and have accepted Dad, Sara, and Rachel as part of our family. However, I claimed everything in the house the moment we moved in, and I won't allow anyone to question my authority.

Second, my skepticism at the initial meeting with the dogs was a clever move to establish dominance and assert my superiority. I'm not unfriendly, but first impressions are important, and I was determined to show that I was in charge. Since then, they've given me the respect I deserve as the ruler of this realm. I've been training the golden-haired canines to follow my rules, and I know they're trying, but it's going to take time. Oh well, I've got time, and they're not going anywhere.

Third, dividing the house into territories made perfect sense. I assigned the dogs to the living room after reviewing the square footage, their sizes, and their daily needs. I even slept on the idea to ensure it was reasonable. Based on my analysis, the living room offered more than enough space for them, so I claimed the rest of the house for myself. In reality, I rule the entire estate, but I let Sara and Rachel believe that they have some independence by giving them one cozy room. The living room is the center of family life, and my generosity should be appreciated. After all, they could have been relegated to the hall closet, and I could always rethink the boundaries.

Fourth, I meant Sara no harm when I bopped her on the nose. If you've ever experienced the unique aroma of her morning breath, you'd understand my sudden alarm as it wafted toward my face. I had to react quickly, so I let instinct take over. I imagine anyone in my position would have done the same I don't mean to embarrass her, but a little tuna juice might help to counteract her breath. If she learned to breathe through her nose, our interactions would be far less tense, given my devotion to cleanliness and order in the house. But what can a cat do?

Fifth, Sara is only allowed to crowd Mom's desk once I'm done lying on her keyboard or otherwise distracting her. One of my favorite pastimes is perching on the edge of the desk and disrupting Mom's work. She should focus on me instead of wasting time tapping on the keyboard—unless she's writing my next book. Despite my protests, she insists on toiling away in front of that bright screen. It makes no sense to me; humans are not the smartest creatures. I've considered knocking her precious screen, keyboard, and laptop to the floor when her back is turned, but I worry it might damage our relationship, so I've held back. Still, if she continues to ignore my orders, I may have to escalate my actions.

Sixth, my toys are off-limits to both dogs. Don't they know not to touch things that don't belong to them? That's just proper etiquette. Naturally, I have unrestricted access to everything in the house because it's all mine. Once, I caught Rachel sniffing Mousey, and I almost lost it. I had to take a few deep breaths and stalk her menacingly until she fled to the other side of the room, finally learning to keep her furry paws off my personal belongings. It hasn't been an issue since.

Seventh, I have dibs on all food, including the dogs' dishes. However, I would never eat their inferior cuisine—unless a particularly tasty morsel appears there unexpectedly. Since it is impossible to anticipate when the man might prepare a special treat for my sisters, I stay alert. I prefer the finely ground chicken, turkey, duck, or fish entrees that Mom prepares just for me.

Eighth, I'm the only one allowed to sleep in Mom's bed. I've even tried keeping the man out by curling up on his pillow and refusing to budge. We often engage in tense standoffs over that prized spot, and I've perfected the annoyed stare for anyone daring to disturb my slumber. If he wants to be near Mom, he can sleep on the floor, but he stubbornly resists. Through careful planning and determination, I'll eventually reclaim that pillow for myself.

Ninth, the climbing tower by the window is my sacred space. It offers a beautiful view and a cozy cradle where I can curl up and bask in the warm sunshine, and it elevates me above my subjects while I nap. It's my favorite spot to ponder life and contemplate the universe. I do my best thinking from that top perch, with the world spread out at my feet. You might even call it my throne, although it lacks the precious jewels and metals that I believe are customary. I'll have to consult Mom and make the necessary alterations to reflect my status in this territory.

Tenth, and most importantly, Mom is mine. I saw her first, and I adopted her long before the dogs realized she existed. My claim on her is absolute, and I have no intention of surrendering it. I love her deeply, and I can't imagine life without her. After all, who would open my cans of wet food? Who would refill my water cup? I certainly won't be dealing with the sink because water outside my cup is an outrage. Mom must remain by my side to attend to my needs and snuggle with me whenever I require attention.

Everyone must follow these rules: handle my stuff carefully, respect my personal space, do exactly what I say when I say it, and remember that Mom is mine. See, they're easy to remember.

Now that you understand the procedures, you're welcome to visit me, offer a chicken treat as tribute, and bow at my feet. That's the normal protocol, but I can be flexible and accept fish treats as well. Arriving empty-handed will earn you a stern stare, and you'll have to give me extra head scratches to win my favor.

I've crafted a perfect life in this forever home, and I've trained everyone to do my bidding. While I become jealous if the dogs occupy too much of Mom's attention, I've also developed an affinity for Sara and Rachel and will allow them to live in my residence for as long as they desire. Don't think I've gone soft. I'm prepared to use my sharp claws and long teeth to protect my family and defend our household. You definitely don't want to end up on my bad side because I'll send my legions of mouse toys to pay you a visit, and Mousey always means business.

## Author's Bio

Leslie Popp is the author of the *Life by Pumpkin* series. Her affinity for writing was ingrained from an early age, starting with elementary school Write-A-Book contests, which she treated as serious literary pursuits. She loves to write about her furry companions and has always harbored a deep love of animals. Her pets over the years have included hermit crabs, guinea pigs, cats, and dogs. Leslie acheres to the belief that pets are members of the family and deserve respect, love, and sometimes their own pillow. She firmly supports the humane treatment of all animals and is committed to a vegan lifestyle.

Leslie Popp

## Rachel's and Sara's Bios

Rachel (2010 – 2025) was a Yellow Labrador Retriever mix with a sweet disposition and a timid nature. Sara (2009 – 2023) was a Golden Retriever with a personality like sunshine and a burning desire to lick any face within reach. Rachel and Sara were adopted in 2016 after being rescued from a kill shelter in Mississippi and fostered on a blueberry farm in New Hampshire. They were thrilled to join Leslie and Will in their forever home in New York City. Rachel's quiet and loving nature led to funny and heartwarming moments as she transitioned from a scared shelter pup to a city girl with many admirers. Sara's friendly disposition and positive attitude allowed her to beguile everyone in her path and capture their hearts. Their floppy ears, innocent eyes, and perpetually wagging tails endeared them to everyone they met.

## Pumpkin's Bio

Pumpkin (2007–2021) was an orange tabby cat with a loving heart and a big personality. He adopted Leslie in 2010 after meeting her at the animal shelter where she volunteered. Pumpkin had been housed there for a year and was overjoyed to find his perfect human and forever home. His curiosity and desire for attention resulted in his many chronicled adventures. Pumpkin had his own pillow and side of the bed, as well as a dedicated coffee mug for water in case the water in his bowl was not to his liking that day. Despite being the smallest member of the household, he ruled the roost. Pumpkin brought so much joy to those around him and is dearly missed.

Leslie Popp

## Synopsis

*The Bark Diaries* records the playful and endearing adventures of Rachel, a Yellow Labrador Retriever mix with a big heart and a curious mind, and Sara, a Golden Retriever with a personality like sunshine and a desire to befriend the entire neighborhood. After being rescued from an animal shelter, Rachel and Sara learn to adapt to their new life in New York City where the tantalizing smell of pizza wafts down every street. The dogs provide advice on handling sidewalk meetings with unfamiliar canines, scouting for tasty morsels, chasing pigeons, and mastering tennis. Rachel reveals her greatest fears, including bath time and stepping over thresholds, and shares her favorite activities, such as drinking from puddles, dancing, hosting parties, and visiting the park. Sara gives guidance on how to beg for back rubs, protest walking in the rain, bake cupcakes, and make new friends. Both dogs offer suggestions on how to deal with the new feline family member, who has boldly declared himself ruler of the roost.

# The Bark Diaries

## Quotes and Reviews

"*The Bark Diaries* is an inspiring true story about two curious pups with hearts of gold who take on the big city. They're determined to be good dogs while searching for treats, chasing pigeons, assisting their dad with top-secret assignments, and showering love on their adopted family."
- Rachel

"This heartwarming tale was written to befriend humans around the world. I have an insatiable craving for belly rubs and treats, and a book seemed like the perfect way to reach a wide audience of wonderful people who can provide both."
- Sara

"The story offers a delightful glimpse into the lives of my two canine companions. However, I must emphasize that it would not be complete without me—King Pumpkin."
- Pumpkin

www.ingramcontent.com/pod-product-compliance
Lightning Source LLC
LaVergne TN
LVHW091539070526
838199LV00002B/128